THE THOUGHTS OF A GOOD MAN

SERMONS AND TALKS OF
DR. JOHN CHESTER FRIST SR.

SUMMARIZED BY

TOM FRIST

iUNIVERSE, INC.
NEW YORK   BLOOMINGTON

The Thoughts of a Good Man
Sermons and Talks of Dr. John Chester Frist, Sr.

iUniverse books may be ordered through booksellers or by contacting:

iUniverse
1663 Liberty Drive
Bloomington, IN 47403
www.iuniverse.com
1-800-Authors (1-800-288-4677)

Because of the dynamic nature of the Internet, any Web addresses or links contained in this book may have changed since publication and may no longer be valid.

ISBN: 978-1-4401-3197-4 (pbk)
ISBN: 978-1-4401-3198-1 (ebk)

Printed in the United States of America

iUniverse rev. date: 3/25/2009

This book is dedicated to the memory of John Chester and Tommy Frist Sr., two brothers who loved and respected each other, and who greatly influenced for the good their families, their friends, and their communities.

INTRODUCTION

John Chester Frist was born on the 27th of October, 1906 in Meridian, Mississippi, the third of the four children of "Jake" and "Jennie" Frist. When "Chet" was only twelve, his father died after being hit by a locomotive. As the Meridian stationmaster, Jake had heroically saved the lives of a woman and her grandson, pushing them off the tracks before an on-coming train. Raised by a loving mother, Chet worked in his adolescent years and attended high school in Meridian where he was Captain of the Football team, "All Southern Guard," and Mississippi's best high school debater.

Turning down an appointment to West Point, Chet attended Southwestern College (Rhodes College) in Memphis where among many honors and positions, he was President of the Student Body, the Honor Council, and of his fraternity. At Southwestern, he decided to serve Jesus Christ as a Presbyterian minister and so enrolled at Union Theological Seminary in Richmond, Virginia. He earned his B.D. and TH.M. Degrees there and later received an honorary doctorate from Southwestern.

After becoming a minister, Chet had pastorates in Moorefield, West Virginia (1932-1937), in Starkville, Mississippi (1937-1942), in Tampa, Florida (1942-1947), and in Mobile, Alabama (1947-1959). It was while he was a pastor at the Government Street Presbyterian Church in Mobile that he died on December 31, 1959 at the age of fifty-three. During his years as a minister, Chet was on the Board of Agnes Scott College and held many leadership positions in local civic organizations and in the Presbytery, Synod, and General Assembly of the Presbyterian Church U.S. He was loved by all as a man of kindness, of good humor, and of principle. The editor of the Mobile Press Register wrote in an editorial that Chet showed Mobile how to live and also how to die. His beloved younger brother Tommy called him "the greatest man he had ever known" and he was also much loved by his wife Betty, and his children Jane, Charlotte, Johnny, and myself, Tom.

Many years after his death, I retrieved these sermons and talks of his from a filing cabinet in the attic of the Government Street Presbyterian Church. Since I was only fourteen when he died, and I wanted to know him better, I recently decided to read through them and then to summarize them so that I could share them with you - his children and grandchildren, his nieces and nephews, and you, his friends. We can all benefit from his wisdom and deep faith.

Unfortunately, in the interest of time and space, I have had to cut them down to their bare bones. I did away with the many stories, poems, quotes, and humor he used to illustrate his topics. This, of course, takes away a lot of their winsomeness. Still, I feel confident that you can get a sense of John Chester's character and teachings from them. The talks come in great variety as sermons, prayer meeting talks, radio addresses, baccalaureate addresses, talks to civic clubs, to firemen, to nurses, and talks to university and high school students. Many of them were typed out with the dates and places where they were delivered. Others were left only in outline or note form. The latter I have just listed rather than summarized.

At the end of this process, I came away with a new appreciation for the depth of my father's faith, for his humility, his balance and practical bent, his sense of order, his humor, his winsomeness, his courage, and his intelligence. I am very proud that he was my father.

Explanations: I first highlight each sermon or talk title in **boldface** and then note the Biblical text reference that he furnished. Following that, comes the first date when the talk was delivered and then, within parenthesis, the other dates when it was revised and given again. From time to time, some sentences are in *italics*. These represent section headings that my father used. At the end of some summaries, there is another parenthesis with an *"S"* that stands for *sermon* and a *"PM"* that stands for *prayer meeting*, with a number that he assigned it. Many talks have no numbers. When possible, the sermons and talks are listed in numerical or chronological order from the earliest to the latest. There are six sections: *Sermons with Numbers, Sermons without Numbers, Sermons without Numbers or Dates, General Talks, Notes for Prayer Meeting Talks, and Notes for Other Talks.*

Some advice: My suggestion is to read the sermons and talks, with their corresponding Biblical text, in small doses as there are so many of them. Some of the messages are similar, but all of them, despite being so summarized, have something to teach us. Enjoy!

SERMONS WITH NUMBERS

"Not far from the kingdom of God" Mark 12:34. 8/9/31 (1/10/37, 7/14/46, 12/18/55). There is a lot of evil in the world, but there is also a lot of good, and those who do good, "are not far from the kingdom of God." To say that we are "not far from the kingdom" is both an encouragement and a challenge. It means that we are on the right path, but also that we have to keep going. Many persons stop at the golden rule or some other moral principle, and do not feel the full meaning of the reign of God in their hearts. *Barriers to the kingdom:* The mind sometimes keeps us out, as Jesus' teachings may not make sense to us. The heart, too, sometimes keeps us out, because we don't want our selfishness and lust to be reined in, or our pride doesn't want us to be looked down upon by others. The will also keeps us from the kingdom, as we have not yet surrendered our self to Christ. Like the prodigal we have to turn from our ways and go back to our Father. We have to become little children in our trust of Him. We are not far from the kingdom, but God calls us to enter it fully. (S9).

"Paul's supreme desire" Phil. 3:10. 11/36 (2/14/37, 6/27/54). Desire is the king of our lives and causes us to act either for good or for evil. Paul's greatest desire was to grow in his understanding of the resurrected Christ and to share in His sufferings. Paul gives us two steps for knowing Christ: *1. To know the power of his resurrection.* Not just to know the historical facts about it, but to know its power in helping us to overcome sin. Resurrection power changes our lives. *2. We must participate in the sufferings and death of Christ.* Only when we are willing to lose our lives for Christ does His power enter us and transform our lives. Paul's aim was to be like Christ and that should be ours as well. We should want to be obedient like Christ, filled with His power, willing to suffer with Him, and to die for Him. (S16).

"It is easy to be a Christian" Matt. 11:30. 2/14/32 (1/12/37, 5/3/53). Most people, men and women, laborers, students, and businessmen, would say that it is hard to be a Christian. Because it is so hard, most of us don't take our Christianity too seriously. For example, for me, it was hard to go into the ministry because of all I would have to give up – parties, dances, owning my own house, not making much money, and not being my own boss. Jesus said that His yoke was easy, but that seems so untrue to most of us humans. Yet there are secrets that make Christianity easy: *A. Looking at life as a whole and not as a part.* For example, the difficulty of refusing a temporary pleasure is nothing in comparison to the joy of having lived a good life. It becomes easier to do good as doing good becomes a habit. *B. Fellowship with Jesus Christ.* It is easy, because we don't see religion as obeying laws by ourselves anymore, but as depending on Jesus for the power to do right. When Christ is the motor of our lives, instead of our selves, then His burden becomes light. (S28).

"Modern idol worship" I John 5:21. 5/2/37 (7/28/46, 1/22/56). Many people believe that we no longer worship idols. The truth is that we do. Our idols have just taken different forms from those of the past. In the eyes of God, our idols are those things to which we give our hearts and loyalty that are more important to us than Him. *Forms of idol worship in our day:* Some worship the idol of the State, especially today in Germany, Italy, and in the Soviet Union. But there can be only one "Fuhrer" and He is God. Some of us worship the material things of this world and money becomes all important to us. Money is useful for doing good, but also evil, and it should never claim our highest allegiance. Some of us worship our fellowmen. We put our trust in human wisdom or in the adoration of members of our families. Others worship the idols of progress, social standing, recreation, and work. *The fruitlessness of such idol worship:* Such idol worship is unstable in its final results. Empires fall and death takes away our material possessions, our honors, and our loved ones. Instead, we should follow Christ's command to seek first the kingdom of God, and then all these things – security, peace, eternity, certainty, necessary material goods, honor, etc – will be added unto us. (S35).

"Doing things we dislike" Matt. 16:24. (5/16/37, 12/13/44). Self denial means life denial and Puritanism to many. Instead, we want to talk of self expression. But Jesus, who says that He brings abundant life to us, also preaches self-denial -- to do things that we dislike. As Christians we have to learn to put duty before pleasure and to learn to like what we have to do. To excel in anything, we most often have to give up things that we like. Having a higher purpose makes it easier to do that. Christ constantly kept before Him the purpose of His life, even when it meant a crown of thorns and death for Him. We must keep our purpose constantly before us as well in order to give our lives meaning. As we do things that we dislike, but that are necessary, we find that our dislikes shrink and a larger world is opened to us. On the contrary, not doing things we dislike, our world shrinks and walls rise up around us. God gives us things to do that we dislike because it is His way of dethroning self so that His love can possess us and set us free. (S36).

"Steps to religious certainty" John 9:1-4. 2/36 (7/4/37, 10/7/51). Worse than being physically blind, is being spiritually blind. That is when we see spiritual truths dimly or not at all. The way to religious certainty is to obey God when we hear Him speak, even in the dark. Sometimes it is difficult to obey because obeying means giving up wealth, position, and comfort. It means doing things that we don't totally understand. But we have to act. For example, we can't understand chemistry without going to the lab. People want to know our experience and not just our theories and book knowledge. The blind man in the Biblical text who was healed, knew only that he could see now. He wasn't interested in the theories and doctrines of the religious leaders as to why it was so. Unlike the religious leaders, he was an honest man with an open and receptive mind ready to receive more light. (S45).

"Your words and their uses" Job 4:4. 8/2/37 (12/11/55). The theme of today is what God does through us in the words that we speak. *Words are not useless, but powerful.* Words are powerful instruments that God has put at our disposal. Jesus said that we would give an account of every idle word and He used His words very effectively. Words can kindle a fire in cold hearts, or kill the spirit of hope; they can open doors to enchanting worlds, or shut out beauty. We affect others greatly by our words. Encouraging words are very important to the growth of character. When we know that others are interested in us, we take more interest in life. Words of faith are needed to tell others of the hope that we have in Christ. God's word, the Bible, helps us face sorrow and trouble and encourages us to go forward with courage. The Bible changes our lives as it did Augustine's and Luther's and the lives of so many others. (S52).

"Wanted – a sense of mission" Acts 22:14, Rom. 12, I Cor. 12. 8/29/37 (6/25/42, 10/3/43, 1/21/51). I once stayed in an apartment in New York City with a Harvard communist and a British traditionalist who taught me the importance of being connected to a cause bigger than myself. Christians also are linked to a Great Power and Cause greater than themselves and have a direct commission to serve others. Christians, however, often lack this sense of mission or call from God. A sense of mission is necessary in life because it makes the smallest task seem important. Abraham, David, and Paul, among many others, all had that sense of mission. So did Christ. All of us as Christians are linked to the great plan of God. We are slaves to Christ. Just as having a mission gave Paul both his message and his courage, so it will be for us. Therefore let us go about the tasks that we have been assigned. (S53).

"A sense of mission – how gained" Acts 22:14-15. 9/5/37 (6/25/42, 10/10/43, 2/11/51). Each Christian, not just the minister, is called to a life of witnessing. All of us can find useful work to do for the kingdom. We all have our roles. *Our first mission is to know the will of God.* We need to learn God's plan for ourselves and for our world, and to be trained in how to carry out this plan. We fail because we try to make our will, God's will, rather than making God's will, our own. Christ first trained His disciples before sending them out into the world. It is through prayer that we find out God's will for us. *Second, we need to keep Christ before us as our inspiration.* We need to do as He did. *Third, we need to hear Christ's voice above the din and competing voices of the world.* If we can do these things, then we can become Christ's hands, feet, and voice to the world. (S55).

"The banishment of self-pity" Phil. 4:11. 11/28/37 (5/18/47, 5/15/49, 11/20/55). Paul was always learning something about the Christian life. In the midst of adversity Paul could say, "I have learned in whatsoever state I am there with to be content." Most of us pity ourselves rather than being content. Self pity, however, is spiritual poison. When pity is focused outward on to others, it is a strength; but when it is focused inward on to our selves, it is a weakness. *We must fearlessly face the reasons for our self-pity:* We pity ourselves because things do not turn out the way we thought they ought to. I had this experience myself this past month with a Tampa Evangelistic crusade which I thought should have been much more successful than it was. We also pity ourselves because of the burdens that we carry. Self-pity accompanies troubles -- material, mental, and spiritual. The way to overcome self-pity in the midst of troubles is to ask sincerely what God is trying to teach us with these circumstances. The truth is that self-pity actually increases our troubles rather than decreases them. It brings unhappiness and bitterness. It steals away courage. On the one hand, life does not turn out always as we hope and expect. On the other hand, the problems and burdens of life can also be used for our good. We will always have troubles, but they will only lead to self-pity when selfishness rules in our hearts. *How to banish self-pity:* We need to learn to meet and use our problems rather than to run away from them. We need to look at the needs of others and spend our sympathy there instead of on ourselves. Paul was able to banish self-pity because all that he did was for the glory of God. Jesus had every reason for self-pity, but all of His work and life was in the hands of the Father. Only when we can banish our own selfishness and immerse ourselves in God's purposes can we learn to be content in all things. (S67).

"Religious concentration" Luke 9:51. 4/2/50. We see the power of concentration in science, business, and education and it is also important in religion. Jesus concentrated His whole life on His purpose for coming into the world. "With fixed purpose, He proceeded to Jerusalem." Paul also had a fixed purpose in his life. "For me to live is Christ." Distraction is a great danger to our spiritual lives and so we must concentrate on our main purpose. *What is that main purpose?* It is to know Christ and to take His Spirit into us so that it is Christ who lives in us. It is to love Him, trust Him, and obey Him. Evil tries to distract us from this purpose by creating doubt in our minds or by urging us to take the easy way, to seek popularity, or to give in to the pleasure of the moment. The way of Christ is a costly way at times, but we as Christians must set our eyes on the task ahead. (S78).

"'Therefore' – the door to Christian challenge" Acts 14:2-3. 2/20/38 (1/23/44, 5/16/48). This sermon is for people who are troubled about the future of Christianity. When there was opposition, *therefore* Paul stayed and preached. This statement inspires us to be daring like Paul. While there is a place for sweet and comforting sermons, there is also a place for challenging ones, such as this one today. Paul faced stoning and beatings, but even so, he still preached. As for us, we have our own challenges, mostly outside the church, but also sometimes within it. Jesus had his Sadducees and Pharisees to contend against, and we have ours – supposedly Christians, but who are living contrary to Christ's word in immorality, cheating, fighting, etc. We must face the challenge to both Christianize the church and to Christianize the world. We are encouraged in our efforts because we are assured that Christ will win in the end. Christianity has always faced opposition and won, so *therefore* let us confront the obstacles before us with courage. How can we conquer? We conquer by being possessed by Christ instead of trying to possess Him. (S81).

"Perfection - the goal of Christian character" Matt. 5:48. (Notes only) 1934 (2/27/38, 12/11/52). (S84).

"Tolerance" Mark 9:33-43. 5/2/38 (6/12/38, 7/17/38, 5/19/57). Jesus shows us how to disagree without being disagreeable. Tolerance does not mean accepting any and all viewpoints, nor does it mean indifference. If we are not careful, broadmindedness can become loose-mindedness. At times we must disagree. Also, there are Christian standards of morality and truth that we should defend. We should always hate evil, but we should disagree in an agreeable manner. There are so many examples of intolerance – the Turks killing Christians, Crusaders killing Turks, Calvin burning Servetus, the inquisition, etc. All of these have caused much suffering. Instead of reacting with extreme intolerance, we can disagree agreeably by respecting the personality of those whose opinions or actions we oppose. Christ didn't force people to become Christians as some colonial armies and even missionaries have tried to do. We must be humble enough to realize that we do not have all the truth, and also we should be willing to learn from others. It is by growing in love that we will grow in tolerance. Love makes all distinctions void. (S95).

"Whither?" John 14:4-5. (A graduation talk at various schools including Peace College). 6/5/38 (1/23/44, 5/25/52, 6/1/52). Jesus always knew where He was going as His goal was to do His Father's business. *Do you graduates know where you are going?* Your beliefs will determine that. Some persons let chance choose for them where they will end up. Others choose a definite path and a high goal, but then don't count the cost beforehand. The result is that they become discouraged and quickly return to a more comfortable way of doing things. Then there are those who count the cost and with determination go forward in the Way and Truth of Christ, no matter the odds. I urge each of you to make that choice. (S98).

"Recovering a note of urgency for the gospel message" Mark 16:15. 8/14/38 (1/25/53). The gospel message spread because of its urgency. To the early Christians, the message was about the only way to be saved. That sense of excitement and urgency is often missing in Christianity today. We have lost it because we have become too materialistic in our interpretation of reality, or because we put Christianity on a par with other religions. We can recover a sense of urgency by realizing the world is full of sin; that the message of the gospel is from the Creator Himself who chose to save us; that the gospel is the only message that will save both us and our civilization; and finally because it is the explicit command of Christ to spread the message. (S103).

"Securing a sense of security" Ps. 62:5-6, I Tim. 6:11-21. 8/21/38 (7/16/44, 1/2/58). The spirit of today is one of insecurity and that is why we have set up all types of insurance schemes. However, the only true security that we can have is soul security. Some persons trust in material things for their security, but these fail. Some trust in their own pride and ability, but these too fail. True security comes only through trust in God. We will never be moved if we trust in the unchangeable God to uphold us in the end. Life events change and suffering will occur, but we will always have God as our Rock and Salvation, and so we will not be moved. Nothing will be able to separate us from the love of God. (S104).

"Peculiar People" Titus 2:14. 10/32 (9/27/38, 2/8/56). We are not peculiar in the negative sense, but in the positive sense of being valued and set apart. We are peculiar because of the price paid for us by Jesus. We are a peculiar people set apart from the world with a peculiar role to play. We are a peculiar people in that we are called to a life of service, not in pride of spirit, but in purity of heart. (S105).

"In the name of the Lord Jesus Christ" Acts 5:17-28. 9/25/38 (6/4/44, 1/9/45, 3/14/48, 11/3/55). What does it mean when we say "in the name of the Lord Jesus Christ?" Sometimes it means that we are Christ's representatives, obeying Him rather than man. In baptism it means that we have died to sin and are born into a new life to become God's sons. In our prayers it means that we can approach God through His Son. Christ is our mediator. Sometimes we use the expression magically, thinking that, by mentioning Jesus in our prayers, we can have our selfish wishes listened to by God. Jesus, however, warns us that simply calling out "Lord, Lord" will not save us. We have to do the will of the Father. (S113).

"Seeking the presence of God" Exodus 33:14-15. 2/2/36 (10/9/38, 6/18/44, 3/8/56). We often speak in generalities or abstract terms that really have little meaning to us. What, for example, does the expression "presence of God" mean concretely? It meant something concrete to David who, surrounded by enemies, could feel the reality of the presence of God with him. In the waters of destruction or in the fire, God is with us even though we can't see Him. He will not fail us nor forsake us. We pray that God will make Himself real to you and to me. (S116).

Life's decisions determine life's directions" Joshua 24:15. 3/16/47 (12/3/50, 6/29/52). We often spend our lives second-guessing decisions that we have made in the past. Too much of this is bad for us as we can't go back to change things. It is most important, therefore, to try to make the right decisions in the first place. There is no place for indecision, because indecision itself can be a decision. Decisions are extremely important as they give direction to life. *How do we make the right decisions?* First of all, we must determine if we want to live a selfish life or one of service to others. Second, we must count the cost of our decisions, as Jesus tells us to do. Third, we should be honest about the real motivations behind our decisions. Fourth, we should be guided by the right principles when we make a decision. Christianity offers us the master motive and right principles for decision making. Like Joshua's call to the Israelites to "Choose this day whom you will serve," Christ calls us today to make the same choice. He also calls us to make this decision without reserve.

If we are to accomplish great things, we need to give our whole selves to Him. (S120).

"Running away from life" I Kings 19:4. 11/27/38 (5/19/46, 10/28/51). Jesus was tempted in the wilderness to run away from life and to not fulfill His mission. We too face that temptation to shirk our responsibilities. *There are many reasons that we run away:* We run away because of cowardice. We run away because we are bewildered and we don't know which way to turn. We run away because we fear that our efforts will be futile. True religion tells us to stand fast and not to run because we are not alone. The Spirit of God is with us. This knowledge turns cowardly men like Peter into courageous ones. The changeless Christ is with us, and He has given us a changeless message in a changing world. Because of His presence with us, we are able to confront change, our bewilderment, and seeming futility with optimism. We Christians are in constant warfare to conquer ourselves and to fight against evil. Even though we sometimes feel overwhelmed in this battle, we must always continue our fight. Christ's strength will work in and through us, and victory will be ours and His. (S130).

"The power of a great purpose" Psalm 121:1. 12/27/52. As we look forward to a New Year, we feel the importance of planning ahead. Our greatness is aroused only when we are able to get out of ourselves and link our feeble efforts with a cause greater than we are. It is only then that the world is changed. We can see the truth of this in the lives of people as diverse as Joan of Arc, Madame Curie, William Wilberforce, Thomas Barnardo, W.K. Kellog, J.C. Penney, and Biblical characters such as Joseph, Moses, and Paul. *Having a purpose is not enough, however.* It has to be God's purpose and not just ours. As we look now to the future, let us make God's will our supreme purpose. In Him, we will find the power to overcome our problems, and we will find the right principles to guide our actions. Our lives will take on a new meaning. Let us therefore give our heads and hearts to God, from whom comes our help. Our purpose is to fulfill His purpose for us. (S133).

"The individual can change society" Matt. 13:33. 9/15/35 (1/15/38, 6/3/45, 6/9/57). God changes individuals who then can change society. Sometimes we are afraid to try to do anything because the problems that we face are so big and we are so small. We say that we are not responsible, but the truth is that we are. Many individuals in the past have changed society, like Abraham, Moses, Lenin, and Marx. But to change it in a Christian way, we need to let God's Spirit work within us. Early Christians were few in number and lacking in power and resources, but they changed the Roman Empire.

Will we let the Holy Spirit take hold of our own lives so that we can change our world today? (S135).

"Escaping our responsibilities" Matt. 27:24. (Jefferson High School Baccalaureate Sermon) 1/20/46 (9/4/49). Pilate said "I am not responsible for this man's death." Like Pilate, we too try to escape our responsibilities. The truth is, however, that each individual has a responsibility for others. Today, the world is looking to the U.S. for political and economic leadership. My desire, however, is to talk about our need to be spiritual leaders as well. People all over the world are tired of the false gods that led us into the destruction of this last war. They want the Truth and bringing that Truth to them is the great opportunity of Christians today. It is our responsibility to bring Christ into our daily work and into our social relations and to spread the good news to others. Let us avoid the spirit of Pilate. Instead of saying "I am not responsible," let us say "This is my affair." (S146).

"Life has a meaning" John 10:10. 3/19/39 (1/29/50). We all want to have a meaning to our lives. Without a meaning our lives are dreary. Some think accumulating material things is their meaning; to others it is the fulfilling of selfish desires. The Christian believes that Christ is the meaning of life. He has come as the Way, the Truth, and the Life. He has come that we might have life more abundantly. He revealed to us that life has meaning when we fulfill the will of God, even though temptation, loss, and sorrow may be our experience. Our view of the universe can give us meaning or give us despair. If God, with His love, is at the center of that universe, then we are filled with hope and meaning. (S148).

"The need of being needed" I Kings 19:4-10. 4/23/39 (4/26/39, 6/36, 4/29/40, 7/16/40, 3/19/50). Revised as "A Need of the Hour" Prov. 20:11. 3/11/56). We want our lives to be useful and not useless. In our world today, neither the very young nor the very old seem needed. But this should not be true. Whatever we can offer in service is important to God – even if that means just being a good listener, a good follower, or witness. Older people can be particularly useful because they have time, experience, and enthusiasm. The world depends on our cooperation with one another, and the church will always need us. (S154).

"The importance of small things" Matt.13:33, I Cor. 5:6. 5/7/39 (4/27/58). Small things can have big influences for good and bad in our lives. We should therefore pay attention to small things. A small oversight can destroy a building, cause a boat to go astray, or can lead to our moral downfall. Small deeds or actions can also have a great moral impact on our lives and on the lives of others. Jesus constantly referred to small things in His teachings like the small loaves of bread that fed thousands and the lost coin or sheep. Little things can become great things in His hands. (S157).

"The Christian Home" Deut. 6:7. 5/11/47 (5/8/49). We often stress the importance of material security in our homes. We want them to be germ free and financially secure. While these are important, spiritual training in the home is even more so. Our homes have become instable with divorce rates climbing. We should pay much more attention to molding our children's character in a positive way, by teaching habits of work and self-sacrifice and by giving them a strong religious faith. Training in a strong religious faith is the basis for a successful person, home, and nation. (S158).

"Thomas the realist" John 20:25. 7/2/36 (5/28/39, 3/7/46). Thomas encouraged the other disciples to go and die with Jesus, yet he also wanted to see Christ in the flesh before he would believe that He had come back from the dead. Thus we see both the loyalty of Thomas and the realism of one who needs more facts before he can believe. Thomas should be the patron saint of scientists! Yet even the scientist must walk by faith and not sight. Thomas is like 'Mr. Fearing' in the Pilgrim's Progress, a burden to himself and troublesome to others. Too much reason and too little faith can lead to despondency. Faith, however, will take our minds above the clouds and disasters that we face and show us the blue skies of hope. A strong proof of Jesus' resurrection is the fact that Thomas first doubted and then subsequently affirmed Jesus as "my Lord and my God." (S162).

"A man's shadow of influence" Acts 8:40. 8/6/44 (3/17/46, 6/17/56). All of us have influence on others through our lives and words. *At times we consciously try to influence others.* Through programs, advertisements, vacation Bible schools, and preaching, we set out to influence people and change the way they think and act. *But there is also the shadow of influence that we have that we probably aren't aware of.* In Acts, people brought their sick to near where Peter passed, hoping that his shadow would fall on them and they would be cured. Many times we have that same sort of silent influence on others. We are unaware of it until the day that someone shares with us how it has affected them. On this Father's Day, we need to consider how our influence affects others for the good or for the bad. After we have died, our influence on others will live on. It is therefore terribly important how you live. You pass through this life but once. (S167).

"For He careth for you" I Peter 5:7. 8/27/39 (5/24/55). Many Christians go through the motions of Christianity, but really, it makes no difference in their lives. But for others of us, it makes a big difference. We feel called by God, we have a purpose, and we know that God cares for us as individuals. The Bible tells us that God cares for us, even though many people dispute that fact because of all the disasters that happen. Some would say that God cares like a general cares for his army – for all as a unit, but not for the individuals in the unit. The Bible says, however, that "He cares <u>for you</u>." God's love for us is greater than any evil. We may not understand everything yet, but we trust that God has the answer. Is the universe friendly or hostile? God has put us in a world conducive to our well being with much more good than evil. History, too, shows us the goodness of God and His interest in individuals. Throughout the Bible we see God's interest in us. God so loved us that He died for us. Jesus shows us that God cares for us. Let us therefore trust Him and work with Him in bringing about His kingdom. (S174).

"My gospel" I Tim.2:8, Rom. 16:25. 9/10/39 (4/28/46, 10/2/49, 3/7/58). What does the gospel mean to us as individuals? How does it become "my gospel?" We can only proclaim enthusiastically what we ourselves have seen, heard, and experienced – not that which is only hearsay from others. To make the gospel our own, we have to think it through. It won't be our own if we agree to it just because it makes us look or feel good or because people in authority tell us to believe it. The gospel becomes our gospel if we start with what we believe and then work outward to things harder to believe. We will find that our belief grows as we grow in our ability to reveal Christ more and more in our lives and work. (S177).

"Self-forgetfulness" Matt.16:25. 10/8/39. A strong, useful life can be built on self-forgetfulness. Self blinds us to the world. Only emptied vessels can be filled. *Self-forgetfulness vanquishes vices.* It helps us get rid of vices such as self-pity, conceit, jealousy, and the fear of criticism. We no longer think of our self as exalted, as diminished, or special. *Self-forgetfulness increases ideals.* When we are forgetful of ourselves, then we can immerse ourselves in something bigger than ourselves. Only then do we bring real good to others. (S182).

"Save yourselves from this untoward generation" Acts 2:40. 10/8/39 (11/16/39, 7/20/40, 4/18/41, 11/5/41). "Untoward" is an archaic word that means literally going this way and that without direction, or dodging around, without an objective. Untoward people go around in circles and are aimless without direction. *How can we save ourselves?* Some say that we need to be like monks and leave the world. But that goes against Christ's teachings, for He told His disciples to go into the world. The secret to the dilemma is to find a constant purpose to guide our lives – Jesus Christ. As Paul said, "for me to live is Christ." (S183)

"Living up to others' trust in us" John 20:21. 11/4/39 (11/17/39, 4/30/40, 7/22/40, 8/28/40, 4/16/41, 6/25/42, 9/26/47, 9/12/58). Jesus placed His trust in His disciples to live out His teachings and to spread them around the world. A driving force in one's life is the desire to live up to the trust that others have in us. More than rules, the trust of others in us helps keep us morally straight. The hymn illustrates it – "I would be true, for there are those who trust me." The people who influence us the most are those who believe in us. God works through trust in His servants - first through Jesus whose one desire was to do His Father's will. Then God worked through the disciples of Christ. Now today, He works through us. (S187).

"Living up to our trust in God" Luke 23:46. 1935 (11/12/39). Trust helps us to banish fear and worries. Jesus trusted in His mission from God despite the disbelief of His relatives, despite His betrayal by His friends, and despite what the world saw as failure. Columbus believed in his mission and despite the discontent of his crew, continued to sail on. We must learn to trust in Jesus as He trusted in His Father. In our lives, we must live out that trust. (S188).

"Making light of our heritage" Gen. 25:34, Matt. 22:5. 11/19/39 (12/21/44, 10/27/53). Men in Biblical times and today are very alike in their character. Esau made light of his birthright and heritage and many in the church today are just like him. They also make light of their Christian heritage, by either disdain or by neglect. Our Christian heritage is of great value and we should not make light of it, but esteem it and build on it. (S189).

"Working Christians," "Doers of the Word" James 1:22-24. 3/2/36 (11/28/39, 12/2/56, 12/9/56). To be a Christian in the fullest sense, we must be doers of the Word and not hearers only. We must build our houses on rock foundations, and not on shifting sand. We all have different tasks in bringing in and participating in the kingdom of God. Those who put their faith in action, in love, and in service to their fellowman, are the ones, whom Isaiah says, find God's favor. Micah calls us to "do justly, and to love kindness, and to walk humbly with God." Jesus reminds us that it is not enough just to say "Lord, Lord" to enter into the kingdom of heaven. We also need to do the Father's will. *Why is it necessary to be a working Christian and to live out the Christian life in service?* It is necessary, because knowledge doesn't last unless it is put into action. We have to apply what we know if we hope to grow. For example, before the walls of Jericho fell, the people had to walk around them, just as God commanded. *You naturally ask, "But what can I do?"* Each of us is to be a witness to the good news, by our words, by our finances, and by the use of the talents that God has given us. Let us only face heaven when our mission on earth has been fulfilled. (S190).

"Christian thoughtfulness" Eph. 4:32, 2 Pet 1:1-8. 12/17/39 (11/26/44, 11/20/49). This is a Thanksgiving and Christmas sermon. Paul stresses that we should be kind to one another. *Thoughtfulness brightens everyone's life.* Especially in the dark days of trouble, it is a light of hope and encouragement. *Thoughtfulness gives incentive to life.* It adds power and meaning to living. *Thoughtfulness makes difficult problems easy.* When you know someone is standing with you, it makes standing for the right easier. *How can we develop this virtue of thoughtfulness?* We can develop it by seeing with our minds, our eyes, and our intuitions the ways that we can best be of service to others. (S194).

"The message of the kingdom" Matt. 6:33. 1/7/40. We can center our values on material things or on spiritual things. Mostly today we center on the material – on getting every toy and gadget and status symbol that we can. *Who are the receivers of the message of Christ?* His message is not directed to all, but only to those who will follow Him. Jesus calls His disciples to a higher life by directing their attention and energy to the building of His spiritual kingdom. That was to be their first concern. We, too, must follow Him, but few of us really do. Instead, we try to live in two worlds, the material and the spiritual, and we fail. Instead of seeking first righteousness, we seek first the material. Seeking righteousness first doesn't mean that we forget the material – getting rid of poverty, providing jobs, etc. No, it is just the opposite. By seeking righteousness first, we would revolutionize the world. For example, a Christian businessman's first aim would no longer be to make money just for himself, but to be of service to God and to others. The same would be true in all other professions. Our first thought as Christian professionals would be to advance the kingdom. (S197).

"Glorifying the Commonplace" Matt. 20:26-27. 12/18/1932, (1/14/40). We want to achieve and be great, but Jesus says that we must be servants to be great. We can't all be at the top, so we should be happy with the commonplace. The truth is that we soon become discontent with our high places and accomplishments, and we will want even more. *God so often chooses the common for greatness.* We see this in the Bible and in life. Some see only a lump of coal, but others see that diamonds and perfume can come from it. Common, simple tasks like farming and washing the dishes, when dedicated to God, can be beautiful. (S199)

"Keeping short accounts with God" I Sam. 15:14. 3/10/40 (3/2/47, 2/29/48). Since Adam and Eve, we have been guilty of *coming up short in our accounts with God.* Ananias and Sapphira are examples of people who came up short, acting out a lie. Coming up short in our accounts with God means that our accounts don't balance with our statements. This is to be condemned. *Keeping a short account with God,* however, means something entirely different from coming up short. It means constantly checking on our relationship with God to see if we are fulfilling our obligations to Him. A long account can be dangerous in finances, in health, and in religion. We need to face our situation day by day and not put things off until it is too late to do anything. This is especially true in our spiritual life. (S209).

"Communion meditation" Phil. 2:6-8. 3/31/40 (7/7/46, 7/12/53, 10/6/57). Why did God enter into our lives and offer Himself? It is God's way of rescuing us from our own failures and those of our ancestors – original sin. Sin is bigger than we are and we can't handle it alone. It is in seeing ourselves through God's eyes that we understand the true reality of sin. Jesus said, "Be ye perfect," but we know that we can never be perfect on our own. But the good news is, that because of God's perfect love for us, as shown in the death and resurrection of Christ, we are saved and made perfect in His sight. That is the message of communion. (S214).

"Worshiping Christians are working Christians" James 2:23-24, Matt. 20:28. 4/21/40 (10/8/44, 9/3/50, 12/2/56). We are called to be doers of the word and not hearers only. Life is not just thought, it is action. Worship must also be action. Jesus often withdrew to pray, but then He came back to act in the world. Works are the outcome of our faith. We cannot just make an intellectual commitment to Christ; we have to become His followers in our deeds. This is what Jesus tells us in His stories and what is emphasized in the Gospels through many examples. We need to examine ourselves and ask ourselves how we are translating the worship of God into active service to God and to others. (S220).

"Stir up the gift of God within you" (Mother's Day Sermon) I Tim.1:5-8. 5/12/40 (5/14/44, 5/9/48, 12/16/56). Never be ashamed to hold on to your mother's hand or to her faith, if your mother was like Timothy's mother and grandmother. Most great men owe much to the training of their mothers. Training and character building is the gift that God has given them through their mothers. We need to fan the flame of the instilled ideals of our religion that our mothers have put into us. We do not want to waste what has been given to us. Not to stir up the gift is disastrous to our character development and to our eternal growth. We need to look back at our lives and see if we have departed from the ideals and dreams of our youth. If we have, we need to stir up the gift of God within us, so that our character and religious life can grow and be fruitful. (S222).

"The goodness of God" Ps. 34:8. 6/2/40 (2/12/50, 6/7/53, 12/12/57). "Is the universe friendly?" is a basic question of life. "Is God good?" *Our incentive to do right and our hope for the future is based on our concept of God's goodness.* We would be miserable without a belief in it. Sometimes we forget God's goodness because of our present sufferings. God does not remove all of our troubles, but He does remove our fear of them. We are told by the psalmist to "Taste and see" God's goodness. It is not by book knowledge, but by experience, that we see His goodness. Also, put goodness into practice and you will see God's goodness. *"How is the Lord good?"* He is good in that He delivers us from our fears; and He is good because, through Jesus Christ, He delivers us from condemnation. "Blessed is the man who trusts in Him." Happy are we if we trust in our good God even in the midst of our troubles. (S225).

"Loyalty to Christ" John 13:37-38. 6/9/40 (2/2/47, 5/23/52). "For my sake" is the secret of true Christianity. Our faith is centered in Christ and our works are done for the sake of Christ. Christianity is not a philosophical creed; it is instead loyalty to the Person of Christ. We may be liberal or conservative, Catholic or Protestant, but loyalty to Christ is what unifies us. Jesus tells us to focus on Him and not on some abstract principle. *The disciples did many things willingly for the sake of Christ.* They testified of Him and they suffered for His sake. Paul counted it joy to suffer for Him and to be counted a fool for Him. Many of us, on the other hand, want a comfortable religion. But Jesus says that we are to suffer for His name. We are also to give in His name; not just our possessions, but ourselves. In losing our lives for His purposes, we discover our real lives. I ask you, *"What are we really doing for Christ?"* Are our beautiful churches, our music, our families, our activities for good done primarily for Christ's sake, or for our own sake? They are certainly for our sake because we benefit from them, but they should primarily be for Christ's sake. He died for us that we might live for Him. (S226).

"Serenity of Soul" John 14:27. 7/14/40 (1/20/52, 3/3/57). Christianity is good news, not about defeat, but about victory. *The world in which we live needs direction.* Our spiritual lives are under the constant strain of defeatism, fatalism, struggle, and war, but Christ promises us His peace. How few people are really happy today. Many wealthy people lack happiness, despite all that they have. *What can Christ furnish a person today?* Christ can bring us that inner peace that He brought to the waves of the Sea of Galilee; that He brought to His disciples and to other followers in the midst of turmoil and suffering. *Where did Jesus get His peace?* Jesus had peace because He never lost His sense of perspective. He saw things for their real value and in the light of eternity. He was not blinded by the problem of the moment, for He knew that God is not in a hurry. Jesus also never lost sight of the God's goodness. He knew that His heavenly Father was greater than any evil or circumstance, and that He was Good. I ask you today to meditate on the 23rd Psalm and its teachings about God. It will help bring you serenity. (S231).

"Grey haired Advice" 1 John 2:15. 8/16/31 (9/22/40, 1/12/56). John was an old man when he gave this advice to the followers of Christ. "Love not the world, neither the things that are in the world." The "world" he is talking about is an attitude of selfishness which is hostile to Christ. It is vanity and all that is controlled by evil. John tells us not to love the world because it is not lasting and it diverts us from our purpose in life which is to love God and His light. The only thing that will last is God and His will. (S240).

"The Christian Extra" Matt. 5:46. (This was completely rewritten two times) 11/17/40 (6/24/45, 1/11/48, 1/19/48). *The Starkville sermon:* We do not accept counterfeits in our lives, nor did Jesus. He had no patience with that which was counterfeit or untrue. He warned against being unfruitful in our lives and in pretending to be religious. He warned against hypocrisy. *We should look at ourselves to see if we are counterfeits.* Has Christianity really improved us? Are we really the salt or the light of the world? Do we confess Him and yet not do what He says? It may be better to openly be a sinner than to claim to be a saint and sin in secret. *The Tampa sermon.* God wants our example to be true, but He also wants our attitude and motivation to be true. We are a people set apart by God, and as Christians, we should do more than others. Our standards should not be the standards of the world, but the much higher standards of Christ. God did the extra for us by loving us so much that He sent His Son to die for us. The love of God is higher and broader than all that we can think or imagine. In our relationships to others, we are also called to do the extra by loving even our enemies. (S253).

"Revealing reality of religion" Phil. 2:15-16. Moorefield, but no date. (12/8/40). Some people do not see the truth of Christianity because of their spiritual blindness; others don't see it because of us who so imperfectly represent it to them. Some people are turned off by our creeds and theology, but most of all, they are turned off by our lives which are so out of tune with our message. Christ became flesh and dwelt among us and showed us the power of God and the love of God in the flesh. The disciples were attracted to Him and Paul was changed by Him. Throughout history, Christians have been transformed by His reality to them. If people are not changed by our message today, it is because we sometimes preach of a dead Savior rather than of a living one. It is because He does not live in our lives as an example to others. The real way to convert others is to have the light of Jesus Christ shining in our lives. Then it will outshine all competitors in brightness and reality. (S258).

"Let a man examine himself" I Cor. 11:20-28. 1/5/41 (7/48). Paul tells us, that before taking communion, we should examine ourselves. It is easy for us to examine and judge others, but it is more difficult for us to examine our own selves. Can we see the spiritual body of Christ in the wine and bread and be aware of the price that He paid for us? What about our obedience and stewardship in comparison with Jesus? When we examine ourselves, we come to realize our unworthiness and our dependence on God. (S262).

"Abiding qualities of life" I Cor. 13:13. 1/5/41. Our lives are full of change. People, buildings, hopes, knowledge - they all die or change over time. Great empires and their founders, like Alexander the Great and Napoleon, have passed away. Change is the nature of our world. Jesus though, the simple carpenter's son, is one person who has remained. Alexander and Napoleon sought false greatness while Jesus sought real greatness, the obedience to the eternal will of God. Alexander and Napoleon founded their greatness on force, while Jesus founded His on love. The people in the church of Corinth, that Paul addresses in our text, sought greatness and uniqueness in their spiritual gifts, and they found fault with those who were different from them. Paul saw the foolishness of all of this. He saw that the only gifts that are lasting are Faith, Hope, and Love and the greatest of these is Love. These are the only things that will survive our transition to heaven. Faith remains because it is Trust in God. Hope in heaven is that we will come ever closer to knowing the Father and to being like Jesus Christ. Love is the greatest thing, however, in heaven and on earth. Faith and Hope are means to an end, but Love is the end in itself, for God is Love. All other things will pass away. (S263).

"Perverted Privileges of today" Is. 5:1-7, Jer.2:11. 1/12/41. The Bible is God's word and the most wonderful book in the world. Lessons from 2,700 years ago are still applicable today. Israel was a privileged nation, but unfruitful, giving nothing in return for God's gifts to them. Isaiah and Jeremiah use the symbol of the vineyard for Israel. It was planted and cared for by God, but because it didn't bear any fruit, it was destroyed. Today, the same message is applicable to us. The Christian church today is the branch of the true vine which is Jesus Christ. We have been placed in the right soil and God has offered us every opportunity. But are we bearing fruit? As a nation, we are failing Him in our materialism, our selfishness, in our wars, and in our evangelism. The church has failed because the individual has failed. *What are we as individuals doing for Him?* In our church we have three and five talented men who live as if they had one talent. Let us prune our dead branches and get back to the true vine of Christ. Pruning hurts, but it is the only hope of Christianity. (S265).

"Lack of interest in missions" John 14:6. 1/10/41. Our missionary program today is in a bad way. What is the cause? *Are our missionaries in the field mediocre?* No, they are leaders of the church who are doing a very good job. *Is the problem insufficient money with which to send missionaries?* No, while giving is down for missions, it is not because individuals in our church have less money. The cause is deeper. *Is the cause indifference?* Yes, we are indifferent, but that is still not the cause. *The cause is lack of motive.* The doors are open around the world, but we do not go through them because we are not convinced that Jesus is *the* Way, *the* Truth and *the* Life and that no man comes to the Father except through Him. If we have no desire to share the good news of Christ with others, then that must mean that the good news means little to us. If Christ is central to us then His command to go into all world as missionaries should also be central. We should obey. (S266).

"How does the Holy Spirit work through us in the lives of those who are indifferent?" (Just notes) 1937 (9/13/42). (S372).

"Failure to accept individual responsibility" Ezekiel 18:20. 3/16/41. In all times, from Adam and Eve on, people have tried to place the responsibility for their sins and shortcomings on others. Doing so makes us into weaklings and liars. *When we accept our responsibilities, things begin to happen.* In realizing our own responsibilities, we acknowledge our sins, we confess our sins, we repent of our sins, we turn from our sins, and Christ forgives us of our sins. We have a new life. (S279).

"Thy kingdom come—but not now" Matt. 6:10. 3/23/41 (10/30/41, 3/12/47, 3/21/48, 1/1/55). We need to have a vision before we accept responsibilities. Our prayers call for God's kingdom to come, but our practices say, "Not now." We want a delay because God's kingdom means giving up our selfishness. *What is the kingdom of God?* It is God's reign in our hearts. In God's kingdom, love would rule our hearts, justice would be the norm, and all men would be brothers. The kingdom means obeying God. *Why do we put it off?* We don't want to give up our pet sins. We don't want to give up our selfishness. In the church we can continue in selfishness, but in the kingdom we can't. We want *my* kingdom rather than God's kingdom. The kingdom of

God must first begin with changes in us. Is Jesus living in your heart? If so, the kingdom has come. (S280).

"Personal Evangelism" John 1:41. 4/20/41 (4/22/41, 6/15/41, 11/3/41, 12/1/41, 10/8/44, 10/17/48, 2/7/54, 3/15/55). The purpose of the church is to take the good news of Christ's saving grace to the world. Personal evangelism is presenting the gospel to all in such a way that all will commit their lives fully to Jesus and decide to live their lives fully in relationship to others. *Personal evangelism means getting personal.* There are three types of church members: those who join because it is the popular thing to do; those who join because the church to them is like a club; those who join because Christianity is a vital part of their lives. There are also three types of ministers: Those who become ministers because their parents wanted them to; those who see the ministry as a secure way of life; and those who feel God's vital call to preach the word. Two of the groups mentioned will increase the size of the church, but the third group will increase the size of the kingdom. Many of us have trouble with personal evangelism because we ourselves haven't felt God's salvation in our lives. Not only ministers, but each person who is a follower of Christ, is called to personal evangelism. It is our personal contract with Christ. Businessmen and other workers can reach people that preachers can't. (S285).

"Practical methods of personal evangelism" Ecc. 11:6. 4/20/41 (11/4/41, 2/24/46, 10/24/48, 3/15/55). Many examples are given of personal evangelism in the sermon. None of us are in the evangelism army reserve. We are all called to the active duty of evangelism. Individual to individual evangelism is the strongest type of evangelism and all of us need to say a good word for Christ in all of our social contacts. First, we should be prayerful so that we learn to be tactful. We also need to learn how to turn our conversations to Christian subjects. We can use opportunities that arise in our business or professional lives for many types of witnessing. If we feel uncomfortable talking with people, we can write letters and we can also invite people to church. (S286).

"The church and false witnesses" Mark 14:56. 3/11/34 (4/26/41, 3/20/55). It is a great privilege to be a true witness, and a great sin to be a false witness. False witnesses have caused havoc and injustice to Christ, to Stephen, to the early church, to people in the inquisition, and throughout history. Our witness should reflect our life, and our life our witness. If not, our witness becomes false. There are false witnesses in the church today who see Christ only as a moral leader and not as a Savior. Fundamentalism can be a false witness if it only promotes the doctrine of Christ, but not His Spirit. We can also be false witnesses by our indifference to Christ. We will be true witnesses by dedicating our all to Him - our money, our activities, our business, and our life. (S288).

"Mothers day sermon" I Cor. 13:7. 5/11/41. Mothers, at their best, display many Christian virtues. They are encouragers. They show faith, as they believe in us, their children. Most of all, they show us sacrificial love. Many mothers are our first image of God's love for us. (S291).

"The understanding heart" Ezekiel 3:15. 5/25/41 (6/25/44). "Next to love, sympathy is the divinest passion of the human heart." Some moral people lack sympathy. Sometimes, sympathy is gained by passing through life experiences that are similar to the ones passed through by others. Many persons in the Bible and in history have left high places in order to serve and to suffer with the poor. Christ Himself became a man and suffered and was tempted as we are so as to be able to sympathize with us. Sympathy is not self-pity transferred to another. Nor does it mean being dishonest with the facts. To have true sympathy, we must be able to understand our own weaknesses. That way we will be able to understand the weaknesses of others. Sympathy is not just a feeling. It is an act of sharing our experience and resources with one for whom we feel sympathy. (S293).

"The paradox of man" Psalms 8:4. 5/25/41 (9/12/43) "What is man that Thou are mindful of him?" The Bible speaks of man as depraved, but also as a child of God. The story of man is one of conflict with evil in his heart, and with his inability to overcome it. *Let us look first at the smallness of man:* Against natural wonders and natural disasters, against the backdrop of the universe or as an individual in a mass of humanity, man is very small indeed. We feel small in comparing ourselves with others who are smarter, more moral, and more lovely than ourselves. We feel small when we falsely accuse others. We feel small, too, because, like the rest of humanity, we are so selfish and do so many evil things. Sometimes we are worse than animals. *The greatness of man:* Man is great because he can control part of the world of nature and can bring justice and progress to the world. He is important enough to God for Christ to take on a human body. Even though, we like Paul, see ourselves as the chief of sinners, we like Paul, should also press on so that we might know Christ and become more and more like Him. (S294).

"Pigeon-holing our privileges" Matt. 11:20-24. 2/25/45 (12/9/51). Jesus upbraided the cities that had rejected His miracles and message. We too, in our indifference to the message of Christ, need to be upbraided. *We have so many privileges.* We too, like Chorasin and Bethsaida have seen the miracles of Christ and have been privileged in so many other ways, yet we pay little attention to Christ's message. So many of our privileges in America - in education, services, freedom and opportunities - in reality, originated in the teachings of Christ. In our churches we have religious freedom, peace, the privilege of Christ's word and salvation, and the privilege of sharing it with others. *The disgrace of not valuing our privileges.* During the week, few of us Christians really live by our Christian principles. Nor do we take advantage on Sunday of the freedom to worship that we have. For example, only about 285 of our 1400 members participate actively in the Sunday School program of our church. *We face judgment for not valuing our privileges.* The cities of Chorasin and Bethsaida were judged and lost their privileges because they didn't value them. We must not let that happen to us as well. We must ask ourselves what we are doing with our privileges. Are we using our training and knowledge to serve others and to bring hope to them? "Have we taken all and given nothing in return?" Shall our judgment be "woe unto you," or shall it be "well done, good and faithful servant?" (S339).

"Joshua – the man of patience" Joshua 1:1-9, Heb. 10:36. 4/19/42. The heroes of the Old Testament show us that we can have an intimate relationship with God despite our failures. When they repented, God forgave them. Joshua receives less attention from us today than many of the characters in the Old Testament. Perhaps it is because he had so few faults and therefore isn't as "interesting" as some of the others. Joshua did have virtues, among them those of courage, obedience, and faith. He also had patience, waiting for 40 years as Moses' assistant until he was given the direction of God to lead the people into the Promised Land. God spoke to him and he was able to do the greatest feat possible, to stop the sun and moon in their paths. Joshua trusted in God to reveal His will to him and to the people of Israel. *There are different kinds of patience:* There is the patience to outlast disappointments, and there is the patience to outlast the slights of our fellowmen in a kindly way. Jesus taught us patience by telling us that we should forgive others as many as "seventy times seven" times. Christ also showed us patience with all the suffering that He faced because of His love for us. (S353).

"Salvage or salvation?" Jude 1:24. 6/7/42 (2/13/44, 2/4/51). The text, "Unto Him who is able to keep you from falling ...." is my favorite benediction as your minister. In these days of war, the salvage of materials once thought worthless has become important. The church also salvages lives that have been thrown away - those of alcoholics, of cynics, of agnostics, etc. Unchristian lives have been made into dynamic Christian lives. Jesus tells us many stories about salvage such as the stories of the lost coin, the lost sheep, and of the prodigal son. Many drunkards and "bums" have been salvaged by the gospel. *Salvation is even more important than salvage.* Most of us, however, have grown up in the church and learned its lessons and haven't had to be salvaged. God so far has kept us from falling, as the text says. The work of the church is sometimes salvage, and sometimes salvation, to protect from falling. In my opinion, it is a greater task to save men from committing sin than to save them from its consequences. Prevention is better than cure. The salvaged product is not quite as strong as the original. (S361).

"Does God care for the individual?" Ex. 3:6. 12/4/32 (4/26/42, 1/9/55). Despite the billions of people who have lived, God loves us as individuals. He calls us by name and numbers our hairs. We are all different one from another just as Abraham, Isaac, and Jacob were different from each other. Yet God loves us all individually, despite our differences. (S355).

"The providence of God" Gen. 50:19-20. 2/5/1933 (5/10/42, 12/15/46). God uses our evil actions for good. This is illustrated by the case of Joseph being sold into slavery by his brothers. In the hands of a great artist or architect, a mistake can be made into a design of great beauty. This is illustrated by Ruskin turning a blot in a handkerchief into a beautiful painting. God is the Great Architect and all will eventually fall into place. God's word is the revelation of His plan. As Ben Franklin said, "God governs the affairs of men." (S359).

"Understanding others" (Also, "Judging others") Ezekiel 3:15. 6/14/42 (7/27/47, 6/22/52). John Wesley learned not to judge others' motives when once he accused a man publicly of being a miser when in fact the man was holding back money and living simply in order to pay back debts that he had incurred before becoming a Christian. Wesley was ashamed of himself. Never judge others until you have walked in their moccasins, or like Ezekiel says, "I sat where they sat." *Snap judgment fails to take important factors into consideration:* Firstly, it is hard to judge motives. Secondly, who are we to judge? Thirdly, it is better first to judge ourselves. Fourthly, we are such mixtures of good and evil that it is hard to be accurate in our judgments. And finally, judging does great harm to others and to ourselves. It creates quarrels, institutes divisions, foments heresy hunters, and promotes the view that we in the church are hypocrites. Instead of judging others, we should judge ourselves by the standards of Christ and try to live by those standards. That way we will promote love, unity, and peace. (S362).

"God and the problem of evil" I Kings 17:20. 6/9/35 (8/19/42). Today we will talk about the perennial problem of suffering and injustice, which neither Elijah nor Job could understand, and which we can't understand even today.

Sometimes suffering trains us and brings out our best. While we can't understand the reason for suffering fully, we do know that it sometimes strengthens us as individuals. We also know that our points of view about things are very limited in comparison with God's view. The bottom line is that the Christian believes that a God of Love is in ultimate control and we are to trust Him. Like Christ and the disciples in the New Testament who underwent great suffering, we need to hold on to our hope and belief that Love and Goodness will finally conquer. (S366).

"What meaneth this?" Acts 2:12, Acts 1:8. 8/9/42 (10/13/46, 1/28/51). We are amazed by many things in life including what happens when Christians actually put Christianity into practice. People were amazed at Pentecost in this passage from Acts when people spoke in tongues. What did it all mean? People were amazed, too, in Rome at how a religion based on the life, death, and resurrection of a simple Nazarene, whose persecuted followers were also poor, uneducated, and powerless, could transform that world. Later people were amazed at the transformation of lives by preachers like Saint Francis or John Wesley. The key to why simple people are able to do great things is this verse in the Book of Acts, "But ye shall receive power after that the Holy Ghost is come upon you and you shall be witnesses unto me both in Jerusalem, and in all Judea and in Samaria, and unto the uttermost part of the earth." Through the power of the Holy Spirit, unstable men like Peter became certain of their faith. Paul also became certain, and with that certainty, came the power to withstand persecution and to spread the gospel. Both Peter and Paul knew God by religious experience. We too must seek that experience. Our lives must be based not on doctrines, but on the experience of Jesus Christ. Once we have that experience, we will be forced inwardly to witness to others. Often we Presbyterians live on heroic stories from the past and have lost our own passion to witness. To combat this, we need to regain the experience of the reality of Christ in our lives. Then we will be full of passion as witnesses to Christ, and those who see us, will be filled with amazement. (S368).

"The convicting work of the Christ-filled Christian" John 16:7-11. 9/22/35 (9/6/42). The prerequisite for changing the world is a changed Christian, with the Spirit of Christ within us. *How does the Spirit work within us?* He convicts us of sin, of righteousness, and of judgment and uses us to convict the world. We need to convince and rebuke the world of its sin, mainly by holding the world's standards up in contrast to the pure standards and pure life of Jesus. By showing His righteousness and how His agape love for us conquers sin, we are also convicted. By convicting the world of judgment, we convince others that, in the end, evil loses and good conquers. *Does the Spirit of Jesus speak through us?* If we are to change the world, we must be willing to let Christ change us and fill our lives completely with His Spirit. We must not just be varnished on the outside, we must be born again on the inside and filled with God's Holy Spirit. (S370).

"How does the Holy Spirit work through us in the lives of those who are indifferent?" (Notes only) 1937 (9/13/42). (S372).

"Christ the All in All" Rev. 22:13, Col 1:9-20. (Only in outline) 1942. Christ is the First and the Last and Jesus is conscious of this as He says, "with the glory I had with thee before the world was," and, "Before Abraham was, I am." With the Father and the Holy Spirit, Jesus created man and the world. "All things were made through Him." To Jesus we owe our total trust. (S373).

"What we do to the Spirit" Mark 3:29. (Notes only) 9/20/42. The blasphemy of the Holy Spirit means that we prefer darkness over light. We also resist the Spirit and we grieve the Spirit. (S375).

"Christ's selective service act" Acts 9:15. 9/27/42 (6/8/43, 11/29/43). (The sermon was also sent to soldiers of the Starkville church stationed around the world.) We know of the selective service act that calls young men to battle, but God also has a selective service act that calls all of us to His service. It has been in effect from the time of Abraham until today. As Paul was a chosen vessel unto God, so are we. Abraham, Samuel, David, the disciples, and all of the rest of us are called by God to be His representatives to our generation. We sometimes try to get away from that call, but like in the poster of Uncle Sam, Jesus' eyes follow us. We are called for a purpose and that purpose is to bear His name before Jews and Gentiles, princes and outcasts. It is not always easy to do this as we may be ridiculed. God warns us repeatedly that we may suffer as His representatives, as Paul and so many others certainly did. Yet we must listen for His call and answer it enthusiastically. When He calls us, what is our answer? (S376).

"Jesus the guide of life" John 10:4. 11/1/42 (4/3/55) Throughout the Bible, God gave his people many a guide, from prophets to kings. The preeminent guide for the Christian, however, is Jesus Christ. *Today we certainly need a guide.* When we look out at life we only see a haze and a question mark, especially during this time of war and uncertainty. Our guide must be the one who said "I am the Way, the Truth and the Life." *What do we want in a guide?* We want: 1. One who has gone before us and traveled the road before. 2.

One who knew and built on the knowledge of guides before him as Jesus did on the prophets. 3. One who knows the forces with which we have to deal, especially the forces of evil and of good. 4. One who guides us with authority and inspires confidence in us. "Be of good cheer, I have overcome the world," Jesus says. (S383).

"The great God" Psalm 95:3. 1932 (11/8/42, 4/15/45). Questions about the existence and nature of God are fundamental for us. The Hebrew concept of God grew over time, from a local to a universal deity. The quest for God in the Bible is as important as the discovery. While Greece exalted Beauty, and Rome Power, it was Jerusalem which saw greatness in Goodness. *We see God's greatness in Jesus.* He who sees Jesus, sees God. God is great in His love for all mankind and for us as individuals. God is great also in His humility and in His forgiveness of us. (S386).

"God in man's life" or **"Evading God"** Acts 17:26-27. 1935 (11/15/42, 5/20/45, 3/26/50). God has made us to seek after Him who is near to us. We will not find Him if we are unrepentant, if we are filled with self-love, if we seek other gods alongside Him, or if we are blasphemous. Intellectualism can lead us to God, but it can also keep us from the real experience of God. Intellectualism can be an excuse to hide our sins. The road of service can lead us to God, but can also act as a poor substitute to experiencing God. Serving others is often easier than asking for forgiveness, and busyness also doesn't satisfy. John Wesley was a failure at first in his service ministry until he realized that his own regeneration as an individual had to come first before he was able to effectively serve others. It is not us who serve, but God who serves through us. Religious familiarity also can keep us from the experience of God, and we should never take our faith for granted. (S388).

"Stand still and see the salvation of the Lord" Exodus 14:13-15. (Baccalaureate sermon at the University of Florida) 5/28/44 (6/1/44). Moses tells us that sometimes it is best to go forward by standing still. This declaration seems contradictory, but in reality it isn't. The academic robes of you graduates are misleading because soon you will tear them off to pursue other uniforms such as those of soldiers. Stop for awhile before you go forward and check on yourself. Your graduation is a good time to stop and think through your life and plans before going forward. Too fast a pace may harm us, while pausing and thinking every so often, will give us direction. Pausing strengthens our confidence in ourselves and in God. By pausing, we can see that God is in control. By pausing, we can see that Christ's principles are eternal and that His victory is certain. Therefore, pause, and then go forward. (S389A).

"God in man's life" Acts 17:26-27. 5/20/45 (3/26/50). What does God mean to you? Is He present in your life? The Bible tells us that He is not far from us, yet we so often do not see Him. The unrepentant spirit and the spirit filled with self-love cannot see Him. *Through intellect we either find God or lose Him.* Often we have an intellectual understanding of God, but not an experiential one. We read many books about God, but we don't read the Bible. Intellect can lead us to God, but it can also hide Him from us. *Seeing God in Christian service.* Service doesn't guarantee that we will see God in this life. Sometimes like intellect, service can hide Him from us. Saul, before he was converted, thought that he was doing a service to God when he persecuted the Christians. It is only when we truly forget self in humble service that we see the presence of God. *The church is the means of revealing the presence of God in man's life.* Sometimes the church keeps us from finding God when it emphasizes too much ritual, but it can also help reveal God's glorious nature to us. Looking back, we can see God working in history, through the church's teachings, its missionaries, and its service. Today is the Lord's Day and so are the days of the future. We can find God everywhere if we just have eyes to see. (S394).

"Christ in strange places" Luke 7:34. 12/27/42 (12/24/44, 12/23/47). One day I was eating at a combination beer hall and restaurant and as I ate, I listened to the Christmas carol "O little town of Bethlehem" being played among other popular songs on a juke box. Holy music was in a strange place. *Christ in strange places.* Christ is in strange places today just as He was when He was on earth. Despite being the King of kings, He was born in a crowded stable. Despite owning all, He lived in an insignificant town in the mountains, a carpenter's son. He died on a cross and was laid in a borrowed tomb. He associated with humble people like shepherds and fishermen and with despised people like publicans, prostitutes, and Samaritans. Throughout history and today too, Christ associates with strange and humble people. For example, D.L. Moody, a humble shoe clerk, has had an enormous role in the spreading of the gospel of Christ. Today, we, like Christ, should not limit our Christian message to fine churches, but we should also go out into strange and difficult places to reach others. Strange and powerful things happen to people when Christ meets them in strange places. Strange and wonderful things happen to us when Jesus comes into our hearts. (S395).

"Today – a day of judgment" Matt. 3:10, Luke 12:2, Matt 10:26. 1/24/43 (4/28/46, 3/6/55). It may not be as noble to speak of judgment as of love as a means of bringing us back to God, but judgment is a reality that we have to face. Judgment is a major theme of the Bible and while it is in the future, it is also right now. Judgment begins when our spiritual lives start to disintegrate. We reap what we sow. Maybe it will be many years hence, but the process begins right now. The Christian knows and takes heart in God's promise, that along with judgment, there is forgiveness when we repent of our sins and look to Christ to save us. (S402).

"The Robe" (A presentation of the book at a night service) 1/23/43 (2/6/44, 2/4/45, 5/5/45, 6/21/45, 1/10/47) Lloyd Douglas was a minister who became a full time writer to teach moral truths. The book is about the robe of Christ – what happened to it and the people who came into contact with it. The sermon is a telling of the story of the Robe. (S403).

"Strength in weakness" 2 Cor. 12:10. 2/14/43 (9/5/43, 2/29/48). (We only have the title page to this sermon). (S407).

"Freedom through discipline" Matthew 7:14. 2/21/43 (9/19/43, 2/29/48). Real life is the narrow way, the way of hardship and discipline. This is the paradox of liberty. *Jesus comes to announce to us freedom.* He says that He is the Truth, and that this Truth will make us free. And indeed, because of the influence of Christ on our hearts and social structures, women have received their freedom and so have slaves. On the contrary, it is the person who wants to live as they wish, without rules, who is a slave to their desires. The free person is a disciplined person, as those who have gotten to the top of their professions can attest. The freedom that comes with success is usually through the narrow way of discipline. (S409).

"You have not passed this way before" Joshua 3:4. 3/7/43. Most of you are soldiers who were sent here to Miss. State College for studies. You never thought that you would be here before you received your orders to come. While here, you are having new experiences that you never expected. Joshua led an army of soldiers trained in the wilderness to the gates of the Promised Land. As they entered in this new place, they faced great dangers and great opportunities. You soldiers also face great dangers, and I'm not now just talking about German and Japanese soldiers. As soldiers far from home, you face temptation and the possibility of losing the ideals you developed in your home. Joshua trained his soldiers in the desert by strict discipline and with a vision of the future in the Promised Land under God as their king. You, as young men, should also keep your eyes on God if you are to remain morally strong. Sometimes God's ways do not seem the most alluring of the choices that we are confronted with and so we get off track. Be careful, for you can wreck your lives. Keep your eyes always on God. (S413).

"Fasting and the modern Christian" Matt. 6:16-18. 3/14/43. Rationing in wartime is a form of fasting and almost half of Christianity observes Lent and the fasts involved. Fasting, along with prayer, was a source of power in the early Church. It is an ancient tradition going back to early religions and was a sign of mourning or an effort to placate the gods. Christ fasted, withdrawing into the wilderness to feast on spiritual values. But Jesus had little patience with people who would use fasting to show off how religious they were. Today we view fasting as practical for the physical body (diets) and as a power in political life (Ghandi). We also need to look at fasting in the broad sense of self-denial for a larger purpose. We get numerous advantages from such fasting, but it is important, that in fasting, our motives be good. (S415).

"The renounced in spirit" Matt. 5:3. 3/28/43. People of Palestine longed to be happy and change their circumstances. Jesus showed them in the Beatitudes that it was by changed lives and not by changed circumstances that we achieve happiness. Tonight we will talk of the first of the beatitudes – the poor in spirit. First of all, to be "poor in spirit" does not mean to be defeated, cowardly, despising oneself. It means giving ourselves completely to God in obedience. If we do that, then we will find security and true happiness. (S418).

"Thinking on our ways leads to God's way" Psalm 119.59. 3/21/43 (12/2/45). There are two ways one can follow in achieving an experience of God and of living out that experience. One way is to focus on God and on His creation and work, which testify of Him. Another method is to think on our own ways and on our individual need for Him. This latter type of thinking will also turn us to God. *Those who get the most out of life are those who have thought about their ways.* Most of us do not like to think at all since it is hard work. And when we do think, we don't want to question our way of living. We will think about our businesses. We will think about the ways of others and sow gossip. But we don't like to think about our own life styles. Counselors tell us that many young people accept atheism as a means of avoiding focusing their attention on themselves and on their own defects. *What happens when we start thinking on our ways:* Some of us will see that we are leading selfish lives that can lead to disaster. We discover that our way of life is not satisfactory. We see the sinfulness of our desires, the selfishness of our hearts, and the hopelessness of our worldly ambitions. We despair. That is the point in which we then start thinking about God and how that His way offers us hope. (S419).

"Power through loyalty" Acts 2:14. 11/16/47 (the last sermon in Tampa and first sermon in Mobile) (7/15/51). As a new minister to this church we are now bound together by loyalty. According to students at Princeton, "loyalty" is the most beautiful word in the English language, and as can be seen in numerous examples, it is a lovely virtue. *A successful ministry of spiritual power is dependent on two secrets:* The first and most important is on God's power. The second is the support of one's loyal congregation. The minister and the congregation must stand together for spiritual growth and progress. If people don't put the work of God and of the church first, the church and the minister will have no power. Moses had two men hold up his hands so that Israel could fight well. Your pastor also needs that type of holding up by you, the members of this congregation. Yes, it was heartbreaking to leave Tampa, a larger church and a larger city where perfect harmony existed, but I believed that God had a purpose for you and me in this church. We will fulfill that purpose, if we are loyal to each other in our support. (S420).

"Conformity to the world" Romans 12:2. 4/11/43 (6/25/44). We are to love the world that God created, but we are not to be conformed to the sensuous world of selfishness, evil desires, and godlessness. It is so easy to be conformed, to choose the path of least resistance. No one wants to be out of style or to stand out. Yet Christ tells us not to conform to the world. Christians often conform to the world, seeking social status in their churches, in their numbers, and in their wealth. We should not be conformed to the morality of the world, but to that of Christ. If we are to be the light of the world, our batteries need to constantly be recharged by Christ. (S422).

"The struggle of the Christian church in Germany" 4/18/43. The U.S. is a religious nation with religious freedom. The German church is a state church supported by taxes. When Hitler took power, he tried to take over the entire church, just as he did German industry. Many followed him. The Confessional Christians didn't. Hitler tried to stifle the Confessional Church by censoring news, drying up seminaries, secularizing youth programs, limiting the teaching of religion, forming competing ceremonies and rituals, and encouraging atheistic organizations. The courageous Confessional Church has stood up against these trends. (S424).

"Where is your trust placed?" Is. 28:20. 5/9/43. Isaiah warns his fellow Israelites that trust in their treaties with other nations will not save them from the judgment of God on them for departing from His ways. During this time of war, we Americans are also tempted to trust more in treaties and man's wisdom than in God's goodness. No stability will ever come until we bow before God and seek mercy and compassion in our own hearts. As individuals, troubles often threaten to overtake us and do away with our peace. Sometimes we surrender to them; sometimes we seek escape in pleasure and drink. But the troubles remain. The only way to defeat them is by placing our faith in the goodness of God and in His faithfulness to us. *When we fear, we should call upon God and trust in Him.* Jesus showed us the nature of God and He also knows our struggles, our need for daily bread, our pain, and our despair. The king of Babylon, Nebuchanezzar, built a magnificent city in Babylon, but he neglected his soul and ended up like an ox eating grass. We too trust in the wrong things and think we are rich when we are really poor. We see today, but we forget eternity. The choices are before us. We can trust in the cleverness of man, or in the goodness of God. We can seek earthly treasure, or seek the kingdom of God. We can live for today, or live for eternity. We need to get out of ourselves and put our trust in God. (S428).

"What is that in thine hand?" Exodus 4:2. 4/1942. Baccalaureate sermon . (5/17/42, 5/16/43). Moses answered this question of God to him, saying that he had a rod in his hand. But the truth is that Moses had much more than a rod. As God's appointed leader of His people, he had God's might behind him. You who are graduates today have more than just a diploma in your hands. You have education, experience, and culture. The most important thing is not the diploma that you have, but what is in your heart to direct your life and the values that you put on things. Our sense of values colors everything we do. If your ideals are low, your life will be low. If they are high, your life will be full of meaning. Some choose values that are selfish in nature, like making money just to make money. Others choose values that are high in nature, such as serving others. Everyone has a choice. The church can help us choose the highest values. The church says "Seek God first and his kingdom and all the rest shall be added to you." (S430).

"Overcoming evil with good" Romans 12:21. 5/23/43. War has unleashed forces of evil throughout the world that threaten to overwhelm us. *There are different types of evil.* First there is evil that comes upon individuals for no known reason – sickness, troubles, etc. Second, there is evil that is forced upon us by others, like this world war. Then there is evil that we call sins of the heart, of the mind, and of the body. These are reflected in an atrophied spiritual life, in the break-up of homes, and in the multitude of sins that we commit. *How can we overcome evil?* The world has tried three ways: One way is that of non-resistance. Sometimes it works and sometimes it doesn't. Another way we fight evil is with evil, fire with fire. Some say war is a necessary evil or we would be overcome. But that way of thinking can also lead to our destruction. The third way of overcoming evil is suggested by Paul in Romans when he says that we should overcome evil with good. The extraordinary thing is that while this tactic doesn't always work, it does work most of the time. Evil creates more evil, and the passion for revenge poisons us as well. Overcoming evil with good is not easy because it goes against our natures. But by returning good for evil when we are attacked, and by filling our minds with good thoughts when evil tempts us, we can have victory. We can overcome evil with good by looking for the light of God in others and in ourselves and by acting with goodness as our end. (S431).

"Discarding greed" Ecc. 5:10. 5/7/33 (6/27/43). Preachers should preach revealing as well as comforting sermons. If we are sick, we need to know how to be cured. Leaders of 26 Protestant denominations in a published statement tell us that greed is the root cause of our present economic depression disaster. The Bible tells us to keep away from covetousness which is poison. *The discovery of greed:* We believe in the almighty dollar and greed is in the hearts of men. Christianity warns us against usury and tells us that all we have belongs to God. Greed sometimes makes us lower our standards and principles to get what we want. Greed affects all of our lives, spreading and contaminating. *The disasters of greed*: Greed leads to war internationally. Individually, it leads to the grabbing spirit of Judas rather than the giving spirit of Christ. We are so busy trying to make money that we miss out on life. Greed doesn't satisfy, as we always want something more. *Disown greed.* Christians are in the world, but not of the world. God has given us good material things and minds to use them correctly. We should use our material blessings in such a way that none suffer want. Let Christ, and not greed, be our creed. (S435).

"The value of the individual to the kingdom" Matt. 12:12. 7/18/43 (5/6/51). Some place a very low value on man. They think that we are nothing in comparison with the universe. Ten thousand Chinese can die in an earthquake, and since we do not know them, their deaths mean nothing to us. But in Christ's view, the individual has infinite value. We are all made in the image of God. We as individuals can have an enormous impact on the world, but to do so, we have to be used by God. (S437).

"Whither?" 1/30/44. Where is our individual church going? We are not to be just a social or philanthropic group. Nor are we to be fanatics, but a tolerant people, always in search for the truth. We should be a church that makes opportunities out of obstacles. We should compete with sin and not with other churches. We should strengthen our homes and bring others to Christ. (S450).

"Jesus takes a census" Mark 11:11. 2/20/44. This church in Tampa is joining others in taking a census in the city in order to gather religious statistics. Jesus also gathered information about individuals. Our census is incomplete while

Jesus' census is complete. He knows all about our lives. We cannot hide or run away from Him as He knows each of us and not just a representative sample of us. *What our religious census revealed:* There is a lot of religious indifference in Tampa. Jesus also found religious indifference in Jerusalem. We need to take a census of our own souls. Have we loved our neighbor, been dutiful to our family, been temperate, diligent, humble, seeking the will of God, and have we worshipped Him? We need to see ourselves as God sees us. (S455).

"The man of tomorrow" John 10:10. 3/5/44. The sermon in outline form deals with a vision of tomorrow's man – not only his houses, his highways, resources, etc., but how he makes a home, overcomes the self, and discovers spiritual values and ideals. Without religion the man of tomorrow will bring disaster upon himself. The man of tomorrow must put character before expedience and have a vision of world brotherhood. He must put God first and then God will grant him an abundant life. (S456).

"Joys we often overlook" Phil. 1:3-5. 3/12/44. Paul found great joy in his Christian ministry, even in sickness and adversity. Joy, however, is often missing in our own Christianity because we sometimes see Christianity only as a duty. That should not be so. *Joy is not a passing pleasure,* but is much deeper than that. *Neither is joy perfect happiness,* because happiness is not the noblest desire of a Christian. Joy can be in our heart even when we are unhappy because joy goes deeper than any outward circumstances. There is joy in Christian worship if we put our heart and soul into it. There is joy in Christian work when we stand for the right against what is evil, even when it costs us money and popularity. Joy comes when we do good for others, especially without others knowing about it. *There are two types of church goers:* those who use the church, and those who let the church use them. There is real joy in working for the church and in speaking about Christ to others. Getting interested in our fellow men brings us joy, even though we often also face rebuffs and disappointments. (S457).

"Forgiveness: First word on Cross" (Part of Good Friday service). Luke 23:34. 4/7/44 (2/18/48). It is at Golgotha that we see the triumph of love over hatred. *Man's greatest hope is revealed in these words of Jesus' forgiveness.* Because of these words, we hope that God will also forgive our betrayal of Him when we stand before Him as judge. *In these words we hear man's greatest condemnation.* First, we are condemned because we hesitate to bear our own crosses. Second, we are condemned because we see just how far we are from Christ's Spirit in our own willingness to forgive others for much lesser injustices. (S460).

"Seeing the signs of the times" Matt. 16:3. 6/19/44 (10/22/50). There are people who have eyes, but do not see. We need insight as well as eyesight. Many businesses are ruined because people do not see the signs of the times. *Where are these signs?* The signs are in the attitudes and actions of men and of nations. We didn't see the clear signs in Hitler and Mussolini or we could have prevented a world war. There are also some discouraging signs today in the loose morals that have followed the war. Delinquency is increasing and marriages are being destroyed. Many think that anything is all right if they can get away with it. Many think, too, only of the present without regard for the future consequences of their actions. But there are also encouraging signs. Today, there is more interest in spiritual things. In these changing times, we should always keep our eyes on eternity – on our God who never changes and who holds us in His hands. (S464).

"The great answer" #1 Isaiah 58:8. 7/30/44. The sermon is based on a book by Margaret Lee Runbeck which compiles ways in which God is working today in the affairs of men. *There is the nearness of God in men's lives.* In war, people who never felt God's presence before now do. *There is the miraculous in certain events.* Many also see God's intervention in many of the events of the war. Especially in the evacuation at Dunkirk where so many thousands of soldiers were saved by calm seas and by the cloud cover that protected the troops and boats from German airplanes. (S470).

"The great answer" #2 (continuation of the book by M.L. Runbek which compiles ways in which God is working today in the affairs of men.) 8/6/44. *The place of the Bible in these days.* Verses from the Bible have given great solace and courage to soldiers in the war who were confronting death. *The place of prayer in these days.* Prayer has also been very important for soldiers in the war facing possible death. *The influence of Christian individuals in these days.* Christians have also had a calming and transforming effect on others. A story is told of a missionary on a raft with other survivors for many days and of her positive effect on them. Another is told about Chiang kai-shek and his wife who so influenced his captors that they became devoted followers. We believe that God acts in history in many ways. (S471).

"What makes the game?" (A sermon for the players of two major high schools in Tampa meeting together before the game). Phil. 3:13. 11/26/44. How can we use football to illustrate the Bible? There are references to stadiums full of people cheering on athletes in the Bible. There are also track, wrestling, and boxing metaphors in the Bible. There is not one reference to football, however! But football can help us learn how we can have success in the game of life. *Cooperation is necessary.* We do not play football by ourselves, but with a team, and so we need to rely on each other. There is a diversity of gifts on a team and each player helps the other. The opponent tries to break down cooperation on our team just as the devil tries to do that in our own lives. *Rules and regulations also make the game.* Without rules, life would be a free-for-all without meaning or purpose. *Heading for some goal makes the game.* We need to have a worthy goal that we are trying to attain in life, just as we have one in football. Christianity has as its goal becoming like Christ by overcoming the self, and by achieving victories over evil in the world. Achieving that goal is difficult and requires training and devotion. But success also brings great joy. (S477a).

"Spiritual storms" Luke 6:47-48, Matt 7:21-24. 10/22/44. Many of us in our congregation expressed fear of the last storm as it approached. Some actually experienced loss because of it. There are also spiritual storms that overtake us and beat on our house of faith. All of us have experienced spiritual storms of doubt, disillusionment, jealousy, envy, and even hatred. These blow away virtues like kindness, love, and unselfishness. The Bible is full of stories of people facing such spiritual storms. Cain, Saul, and Judas are three such persons who come to mind. There are also storms in our lives caused by immoral living, and people like King David were caught in their swirls. We cannot escape from these storms as Christ did not escape from them in Gethsemane. We can however prepare for them in different ways: *God's warning offers us time for preparation.* Unfortunately, we often ignore the warning and are unprepared. *We can prepare by building well in anticipation of them.* Like the man who built his house on the rock, we should also prepare well for the coming storms of life by building strong defenses. Well prepared shop owners board up their windows before the approaching hurricane. We have to recognize our weaknesses and do something to shore them up too. For example, if we have weaknesses with alcohol we should avoid it. The most important thing we can do in preparation is to anchor our lives in Jesus Christ. *Beware of the lull in the storm.* When we think the storm has passed, it threatens to become even more powerful. We might have overcome youthful storms of passion, but worse winds of self righteousness and pride can hit us with even more force. We can never let down our guard. *Believe that out of the storm there will come a better day.* We must have faith that, out of the ruin caused by the storm, good can come. It is hard sometimes to have such faith, but we must cling to it. God is in charge of all things and He is a good and loving God. Just as the cross on the church here in Tampa withstood the last storm, so does Christ triumph over all the spiritual tempests that can come into our lives. (S478).

"Circumferential Christians" Mark 12:34. 10/29/44 (4/29/51). Stonewall Jackson was a sensitive and retiring man who became a Christian relatively late in life. He, however, was conscious of his duties to witness, and he did it even though it was hard for him. Too many Christians shy from their duties and stay on the fringes of religious experience. Like the rich young ruler, they are close to the kingdom, but still outside of it. *Forms of circumferential religion.* One type of circumferential Christian is a person who runs from one "ism" to another, or from one denomination to another, always on the outskirts. A second type is a person who finds his religion in his social club or in his work. A third type is one who substitutes his social or humanitarian work for religion. A fourth type of circumferential religious person is the moralist who depends on moral laws and discipline alone and not on a personal relationship with Christ. A fifth type is one who stays in the adolescent stage of religion, but does not advance to adulthood and take responsibility for his actions and growth. Religion should be the wind in our sails, and not an additional burden to us. *Tragedy involved in being circumferential Christians.* Nominal Christians think that they have the real thing when they really have only a part. They don't access the power of Christ that could be theirs. Imagine what our church of 1,400 members could do if all of these members were active Christians! Nominal Christians are not far from the kingdom. All that they need to do is to truly surrender their lives to Christ and stop circling around the decision. Then they will become truly committed, joyful, and useful Christians. (S479).

"The art of saying no" Dan. 3:18. 4/16/50. Some people who can't say "no" have made nervous wrecks of themselves. Sometimes we take on more responsibility than we have the time or talent to handle. *It is often easier in the short run to say "no" to righteous behavior than to selfish and evil behavior.* We end up saying things like "while I agree in principle," or "now is not the time," and then don't do what we know that we should. *It is costly to say "no" to evil, as evil is sometimes viewed as what is popular.* It was costly at first to Daniel and the other two young Hebrews who showed their strength by saying "no." They ended up in the lion's den, but then God protected them. The apostles said "no" when they were told not to preach. *In the long run it costs us more to say "yes" to evil.* Look at Adam and Eve, Lot's wife, the rich young ruler, the prodigal son, and others. Many alcoholics who seek help at the church have not been able to say "no" to drink. *The best way to say "no" to evil, is to first say "yes" to righteousness.* Joseph could say "no" to evil because he had first said "yes" to God. Jesus said "yes" to His Father when He was tempted in the wilderness, when Peter tried to show Him an easier way, and when He was in the Garden of Gethsemane. We should follow His example by saying our "yes" to God. (S482).

"Our coddled Christians" Ps. 106:15. 1/14/45 (12/28/47). Some accuse us Christians of speaking high sounding phrases of love and courage, but then our actions do not correspond to our words. We want only the benefits of Christianity with little of its sacrifices. We are coddled Christians. We don't want to give up our time or money to the church. Our Christianity changes like a weathervane with whatever wind of popular opinion that blows on it. *It is dangerous to wish ease over hardship, for God might grant our wish, but give leanness to our souls.* Too often we wish to be socially respectable at all costs. We believe in one standard for our work and another for our Sunday worship. In Germany, national Christians justified horrible persecutions in order to fit in. We, too, often lower our Christian morals in America so that we can fit in. God allows this, but gives us leanness of soul, and so our religion is without backbone, meaningless, and shallow. We have become overly materialistic in America. *The Christian religion that will win respect from the world is one that has high ideals and that demands sacrifice.* That is the life abundant that Christ promises us. We as individuals must choose and America must choose. Do we want to be weak and selfish Christians, or do we want to be virile sacrificial Christians. "Stir us afire, Lord, Stir us, we pray!" (S483).

"Our weapons at hand" I Sam. 21:8-9. 1/28/45 (1/4/48). David is at a low point in his life. Saul has tried to kill him and he has been advised by Jonathan to flee. Discouraged, David seeks food and weapons with the priest Ahimelech who offers him what he has - the holy bread and Goliath's sword that David had used to kill the giant. This story teaches us two spiritual lessons for situations in which we, too, face discouragement and defeat: *Past victories sustain us.* David found new courage in the sword of Goliath, because it reminded him of past victories against terrible odds. With God's help, he had been victorious against the giant Goliath and against the bear and lion that attacked him when he was a shepherd. We, too, can be fortified by remembering past victories over temptation and circumstance. Out of darkness can come light. *The converse is also true -- past defeats tend to weaken us.* The remembrance of past times of cowardliness and defeat weaken us. In the novel "Lord Jim," the main character remembers a cowardly act of his in the past that follows him in his mind even to the farthest outposts of civilization in Africa. Moral or physical defeats of the past can influence us for the rest of our lives. Sometimes this happens because we are afraid that others will find out about them; sometimes it happens because we are just ashamed.

Each defeat can lead to more defeat and each success to more success. Let us live each day aware of this truth, and let it guide us in how we act. (S485).

"It is finished" John 19:30. 3/30/45. The meaning of the cross is so deep that no one can fathom it. Yet one thing of which I am certain is that because of Christ's sacrifice, we have new hope. Because He came to our level, we can rise to His level. "It is finished" is Christ's triumphal note of victory. That victory over death is why Protestants show an empty cross rather than a suffering Jesus on a crucifix. *This cry was the culmination of all His life work.* The word "it" refers not just to Christ's suffering, but to His whole life-plan and purpose. Christ was there at the Creation, at the Fall, and it was His life and sacrifice that made our Redemption possible. *"It is finished," can be welcomed words in our own lives also.* For example, how wonderful the words sound to a mother waiting for a war to end and her son to return home. Christ's work was finished on that day, but our work will continue until the day that hatred no longer rules the hearts of men. It is only in Christ and His Spirit that we can triumph and the kingdom of God can come to earth. (S489).

"Our nation's Mount Nebo" Deut. 31: 2-6. 4/15/45. (This sermon was preached on the Sunday after the death of President Roosevelt). Life is more dramatic and tragic than we know, and the history of the Hebrews is akin to our own. Moses, after a life of luxury as Pharoah's adopted son, led his people through the struggles of the desert and prepared them for entry into the Promised Land. But just when they are to enter the land, God tells Moses that he cannot go in with the rest of Israel. However, God takes him to Mount Nebo so that at least he can see the land with his own eyes. President Roosevelt also came from a life of privilege, and then served and led his nation through hard times. God did not leave him alive, either, to see the fruits of victory and of peace, and so we must go on without him. *What do we see from our Mount Nebo as we look into the future?* Joshua and Israel saw rough traveling ahead, but also saw the fulfillment of God's promises to them. We too see a rough road ahead because of internal enemies like selfishness and the lack of belief in our new leaders. We see dangers confronting us, such as the worship of the false gods of materialism, of militarism, and of imperialism. But we also see from the mountain a vision of human brotherhood, world peace, prosperity, and freedom. *Requirements for us to fulfill this vision from Nebo.* First, we have to believe that God will raise up for us new leaders to help us achieve the vision of world peace. God is indispensible, but our leaders are not. Second, we must determine to obey God. We can never achieve the Promised Land of peace unless we base that peace on the moral laws of God. Third, we must trust in God to see us through. Let us then work and live for peace. (S491).

"The church militant" Eph. 6:12. 2/13/55. Paul liked to battle and the words "strive," "fight," "overcome," and "conquer" are part of his language. We too enjoy good battles in sports, in fighting disease, and in business. One of the weaknesses of some brands of socialism is that they don't take into account man's competitive spirit. Religion also capitalizes on this spirit of man to fight and conquer when faced with evil. But it is important in this fight against evil that we follow Christ's rules and arm ourselves with His Spirit. It is also important to fight the right foe. The first foe we have to struggle against is ourselves. When, with God's help, we conquer self, we are well on the way to establishing God's kingdom. Conquering self, we become useful tools that God can use. The second foe we need to fight against is the social evils of the world. They must be done away with if a more just society is to emerge. The third foe is the demonic powers of evil that face us. Our battle will never end in this life, but we know that we will have eventual victory if we are clothed in the armor of Christ. (S499).

"What does Christianity offer?" Eph. 3:8-9. 9/16/45 (6/20/48, 2/14/54, 12/15/57). We all want more out of life. Some of us seek gold as a means to make our lives bigger and better. Some seek power as the key to expanding our lives. Others seek thrills of every kind. We search for an abundant life in education, business, technology, psychology, and philosophy. Some discoveries help, and some bring us to despair. The Church thinks that it has the answer to how we can have a bigger and better life. Paul preaches the "unsearchable riches" of Christ. What exactly does Christianity offer? *It offers new life itself.* It offers us a chance to become new creatures, with a new relationship to God and a new reason for living. But before that is possible, we have to come to the end of our rope, admit our sin, and submit to Christ. *Christianity offers us a new outlook.* We all face hardship, sickness, and sorrow, but Christianity gives us a new outlook on them and the assurance that in the end we shall overcome. As Christians, we see others as our brothers and sisters. While once we were defeated, we now find new strength and courage. (S500).

"The A.B.C. of Christianity" I John 1:3. 11/17/46 (12/7/47). In brief, what is our Christian faith? *The "A" of Christianity is the Authority of God's word.* Christianity is a revealed religion. We believe that through the Bible, God reveals Himself to man. The Bible also reveals to us the needs of our inner life and the needs of the world, and shows us the way to victorious living. *The "B" of Christianity is the Broadness of God's love.* The very heart of the Christian message is the good news that God is Love. Whosoever believes in Jesus will have eternal life. That means you and me. Being a minister can never be dull when you can offer to people in sin and despair the love, the mercy, and the forgiveness of God. We fallible human beings sometimes forget just how broad God's love is for us. It is offered to all of us, no matter what our race or class. *The "C" in Christianity is the Completeness of Christ.* Christ, who is perfect in all ways, is the cornerstone of our Faith. He is the First and the Last, the Word who was in the beginning and the final Judge of all. Let us spread to all this simple message of Christianity. (S602).

"A new name" Acts 3:15. 9/29/46 (3/28/48, 2/1/53). There are many wonderful names given to Christ in the Bible such as the "Son of God," the "Son of Man," the "Son of David," the "King of the Jews," the "Prince of Peace," etc. But this new name, the "Pioneer of Life" is one of the most descriptive. Jesus is the One who goes before us to show us the way, the truth, and the life. *He is a Pioneer concerning world understanding and brotherhood.* With our world getting smaller because of transportation and communication, the task before us is to promote world understanding. We are destined to destruction if we don't learn to live together in peace. To live in peace, we must share a common ideal to hold us together. In Christ, the world can find a common leader. Christ can rally people as diverse as Luther and Loyola, Moody and St Francis. *He is a Pioneer concerning the morals of men.* Jesus was a pioneer in teaching us how to live. He taught eternal principles rather than rules. He taught that first we should seek the kingdom of God and to love God with all our heart and our neighbor as ourselves. We don't overcome our sin and weakness through obeying rules, but by being filled with love. *He is a Pioneer concerning the very meaning of life itself.* We find meaning in life by attaching ourselves to the Highest and to the Whole rather than to some lesser god or inferior purpose. Christ has gone before us to prepare the way – to show us new life, to overcome temptation, to be resurrected to new life. He is the Captain of our souls. Let us trust Him and follow Him, even though we are yet far away from being like Him. (S610).

Sermons without Numbers

"Be steadfast in life" 2 Cor. 6:1-18. (Eastland Church, Memphis) 3/28. In the face of persecution, Paul calls the Corinthians to be steadfast and courageous. He wanted them to know that it is better to die for Christ than to live without Him. Christians are found all over the world because missionaries were steadfast when they faced persecution, whether it was by public opinion or death. Christianity requires real men. Jesus was love and gentleness itself, but He was also strong, fearless, and steadfast.

"The resurrection" I Cor. 15:17-18. (Eastland Church, Memphis) 4/28. The resurrection of Christ is a fact but let us suppose tonight that it is not true. What would the world be like and our lives be like if He had not risen? There would be no Easter and our religion would be meaningless and the world would still be in the darkness of sin and despair. Paul says, "And if Christ be not raised, your faith is vain, ye are yet in your sins." The resurrection is the one thing that makes Christianity different from other religions. Imagine the dismay of the disciples and of Paul and the early Christians if it were not so. They were so convinced of the resurrection that they faced terrible sufferings to spread the good news of hope. The thought gave them joy because it meant that life conquers death and goodness conquers evil and sin. How dark and vain would their lives be were it not so. But the good news is that it is so. Jesus did rise from the dead, and according to Paul and to other gospel writers, He appeared to hundreds of people who could vouch for the fact. The resurrection of Christ is a fact in history, but is it a fact in your life? Without Christ living within us, we are of little value. With Him in us and leading us with His power and grace, we have the "hope of glory." On this Easter night, should we not rejoice to know of the victory of Christ and of all of those who accept Him as their Savior and King? Are we ready to accept Him tonight?

"Sow happiness and reap happiness, etc." Gal 6:7. (Eastland Church, Memphis) 5/28. When Gypsy Smith preached in my home town of Meridian on the text "Be not deceived, God is not mocked, whatsoever a man soweth that will he also reap," many people repented after examining their lives and seeing all the bad things they had done. Tonight, I want to focus on the other side of the passage. Instead of sowing evil and reaping evil, let us think of sowing kindness and reaping kindness, of sowing goodness and reaping goodness, and of sowing the Christian message where ever we go, and reaping the sheer joy that can be found in such work. Jesus said, "Seek ye first the kingdom of heaven and His righteousness and all of these things shall be added unto you." This is advice and not a warning. It brings love rather than fear into our hearts. Paul tells us that "the kingdom of God is not meat and drink, but righteousness, and peace and joy in the Holy Ghost." The kingdom of God must be in our own hearts before we can spread it to others.

"Man and his money" I Cor. 4:2. 3/6/1932 (3/3/37). When a crisis happens, it can teach us the true value of things. During this time of depression, the work of the church is threatened because it is sometimes put on the back burner in our finances. *Even in bad times, the gospel should come first.* God should be our partner in the acquisition of money (right jobs), in the saving of money (not hoarding), the spending of money (to meet real needs and to advance us spiritually), and in the giving of money (generously for God's kingdom). John Wesley said, "Earn all you can, save all you can, give all you can." Looking at money in this way will bring us joy.

"The widow's mite" Mark 12:4. 3/12/1933. We need money to advance the kingdom of God on earth. In Moorefield, the distinctions between wealth and poverty are not nearly as great as in the Biblical story. Here in Moorefield, almost all are suffering financially with this depression, facing high taxes on land and no place to sell our products. The widow in the story gives not out of duty or desire to be seen and praised, but she gives out of love. We Christians are sometimes unhappy because we have not surrendered our lives totally to God. This holding back from Him reflects in our giving because we often give grudgingly. Jesus is concerned about how we make and use our money as well as about the spirit of our giving.

"Christianity and the home" Deut. 6:6-7. 5/14/33. During this time of depression, the President and Congress are focusing their efforts and our money on saving homes because our homes are the economic and moral backbone of the nation. Heredity and environment shape us in the home. The examples and teachings of our parents mold us. Keep Christ as the center of your home and it will be a place of happiness.

"Building palaces from broken plans" Gen 45:5-8. 12/33 (1/28/34, 11/8/42, 10/20/57). Like the stained glass window craftsman who takes broken pieces of colored glass to make a magnificent window, we too can take broken dreams and reshape them into something beautiful. Sometimes they are dreams for our selves, sometimes they are dreams for our children. Life is a continual readjustment from one broken dream to another. Joseph in the Bible is a great example of one who made a palace from broken dreams. Joseph was the choice son of a rich family, and then one calamity after another happened to him. He was sold into slavery, forced to leave his land and his father; he was lied about, put into prison, and forgotten. But he took these events and became the second most powerful person in Egypt. How did Joseph do that and how can we make something of our broken dreams and plans? *He conquered the situation rather than letting the situation conquer him.* Sometimes what looks to us as defeat can be the ingredient for future success. *Joseph never lost sight of his higher visions.* He had inner strength and held on to his morals, his belief in his fellowman, and his ideals. *Joseph never lost sight of his God who was working in and through him for higher purposes.* It was a trust in God that never failed. He built his palace upon a foundation of belief in God who was with him and showed him kindness. Here is where we Christians have an advantage over others. Troubles may come to us, but we are not alone. God is with us and we can do all things in Christ who strengthens us. We believe that all things work together for good for those who love God and are called according to His purpose. Paul is the New Testament image of Joseph. He too was in chains, but these chains worked out to the good for his work in Christ. With God as the foundation of his life, nothing could defeat him. God, too, is at work in us. With His guidance, let us build palaces from our broken dreams and plans.

"Experiential knowledge of Christ" II Timothy1:12. (Notes only). 11/24/34 (11/29/33, 9/24/34, 10/25/35, 3/16/36, 6/8/37, 10/16/38, 11/39, 7/22/40, 4/17/41, 10/29/41, 6/10/43, 9/9/45, 4/20/50). It is one thing to believe that God exists; it is quite another to feel His reality in our lives. Paul believed in a Person and not so much in creeds and laws. We learn to know Christ by obeying His laws and working with Him. His law is the law of love. Doing something loving in the name of Christ is much better than just reading philosophy. Just as we see God in His works, others should see Christ in us. Job says, "I know whom I have believed," and Paul says, that for him to live is Christ.

"Looking at yourself in a mirror" James 1:23-24. 9/24/39 (11/14/39, 4/30/40, 7/18/40, 4/14/41, 6/24/42, 9/28/58). *We are a mirror-looking* *generation.* We spend millions of dollars to make our outward appearance look pleasing, to hire psychologists, or to buy self-help books to tell us about ourselves. This can be money well spent if it makes us, like the prodigal son, turn from our ways and towards God. *We are also a generation which asks ourselves questions.* Like the prodigal, we need to ask ourselves why we are where we are, and what we should do to return home. It is good to look at and talk to ourselves if it will help us understand who we are. However, the crucial thing is to use that information to change our lives. James has it right when he says that we look at ourselves in a mirror and then go away forgetting what type of persons we are. In other words, we take no action. This is where we and the prodigal son are different. The prodigal son took action to change his situation, and sometimes we don't. The danger in our evangelistic services is that after we see our sin and decide to change, we don't put our decision into practice. *We must not only see and say, we must act.* Once, a man said to Mark Twain that he was bothered by the things in the Bible that he didn't understand. Mark Twain replied that he was bothered by what he did understand. The commands of Jesus are sometimes difficult, and so we choose not to follow them. And that is our problem.

"Why men do not believe" Mark 9:24. 11/29/41 (11/30/41, 1/18/53, 3/16/58). Most of us repeat our creeds over and over without really believing the words we say. That is why our faith has so little power. When Jesus did miracles, the humble saw in them the grace of God, while the Pharisees saw the power of the devil. *Why people still do not believe.* There are those who don't believe because they have never heard the good news. There are those who don't believe because they are atheists and see all life and events as chance. Then there are those who have honest doubts. The latter will one day find the truth if they continue their quest in sincerity. One such man was the subject of our text. "Lord, I believe, help Thou my unbelief." Belief comes hard to some, like it did to Thomas in the Bible. A fourth class of unbelievers is those who live as if belief is unimportant and unnecessary. They are indifferent. These are the ones who worry me the most. They assent intellectually to a creed, but it never actually changes their conduct or colors their thinking. They affirm a creed, but just do not care to practice it. These types of unbelievers are in the church and outside of the church. *Why then will these not believe?* The truth of Christ has been presented to them and confirmed by the experience of the church, but they still don't believe and live by those beliefs. The pull of worldliness keeps some from believing, as the god of this world has blinded them. Day after day we are seduced by the pleasures and gaudy toys and values of the world. Some of us are living in such a way that we don't want to hear the truth. Accepting it is too costly for us. It will mean that we will be called to give up ways and things that we want desperately to hold on to. We don't want to hear that we are sinners. What is keeping you from saying with whole-hearted sincerity, "I believe?" What is keeping you from living by the power of your faith? Since we have all the evidence we need of the victorious life of Christ, is it because of secret or outward sins, because of selfishness and pride, or because of commitment to the status quo? We need to live by the power of the faith that is ours.

"Guidance of God" John 16:13, Is. 30:21. 10/25/42 (2/23/47, 4/9/47, 10/16/55). Do you think that God really guides and cares about the individual? Many leaders fall on their knees looking for God's guidance before they make major decisions. Many of our hymns speak of God's guidance like "Lead kindly Light," "He leadeth me," "Guide me, O Thou Great Jehovah." *We sing about God's guidance, but do we practice it?* Both Old Testament and New Testament writers urge us to seek God's guidance. As James says, "If any of you lack wisdom, let him ask of God who gives to all liberally." *What do people say about God's guidance?* Some wonder how the infinite God could be interested in us as insignificant individuals. Some see God as a commander in chief interested in the final outcome of the battle, but not in the lives of each private. Christ says, however, that God is interested even to the point of counting the hairs on our head. Experience proves that this is true. *What natural avenues does God's guidance take?* God works through natural as well as supernatural means. One mean is common sense. Sometimes circumstances guide us. Sometimes failures lead us to another direction. Sometimes it is other people who give us advice. *What supernatural avenues does God's guidance take?* God uses his Divine Word as a light to us, as well as the promptings of the Holy Spirit. We are told that "the steps of a good man are ordered by the Lord." Constant persevering prayer will bring us into contact with this guidance of God. But guidance is not all that we need. We need also to follow the guidance that we receive. The promises of God are true, and Jesus promised that the Holy Spirit would guide us as our Comforter and Encourager. Let us accept this truth and live by this great thought.

"Tackling life" 2 Cor. 10:2. 11/8/45. (A sermon full of illustrations for the Hillsboro and Plant Football squads). Fishing was the main sport in Jesus' time, so many of His messages were built on fishing metaphors. Today football is popular, so let us build a message on it. According to Moffatt's translation of the text of today, Paul says, "My mind is made up to tackle certain people." Like Paul we need to learn to face up to our problems and tackle the circumstances of life as we meet them. *The fundamental principles of real living:* We need to know the fundamentals of football and of life and practice them. Tackling is one of them. *Must tackle the problem of real sportsmanship.* We must play the game of football and of life hard, but fairly, following the rules. *Must tackle the problem of being a winning loser.* The fact is that we cannot always win our games, and we must learn to become gracious losers who can learn from our defeats. This will make us into stronger players. *Must learn to tackle personal living.* To be a good player in football or in life, we must train constantly and lead a clean life. We also must not let the praise of the crowd go to our heads. *Life is not tag football.* We can't play life as if it were tag football. We have to face up to and tackle the problems before us if we want to be a success. We are as big as any problem we face if we tackle it with all that we have.

"The gift of new life" Matt. 1:25. 12/23/45. The birth of Jesus lifted men and women into another world that they had never known before. In this new world, the spiritually blind were brought to sight, the heavy burdened were given peace, and those overcome by evil became pure. *He lifted us to a new moral world that was not natural according to our original human nature.* With the Sermon on the Mount, Jesus called us to live by high principles rather than by laws and rules. He brought inner as well as outer purity to us. *He lifted us to a new world of better understanding of ourselves.* Jesus knew what was in our hearts. He knew the evil, but He knew also that the Spirit of the Divine was in us. Jesus gave us new dignity because He told us that God loves us and Christ's Spirit has spread compassion in our hearts and taught us to love others. *He lifted us into a world whereby we come to know God as a loving heavenly Father.* Jesus revealed God's nature to us as a loving heavenly Father who cares for our world and for us as individuals. He taught us that God has a purpose for each of us and that that purpose will surely be fulfilled. Because of Christ, we understand ourselves better, our fellow man better, and God better. We want to share with others our new understanding.

"Tired people in trying times" Mark 14:37-38. 3/3/46 (3/13/47, 3/26/50). After a very physically and psychologically trying week in Jerusalem, Jesus and the disciples are in the Garden of Gethsemane. Jesus returns from praying His agonizing prayers, and when He needs the support of His disciples the most, He finds them asleep. *Today is a momentous time in the history of the world.* The world today is going through great changes in Japan, China, and India, as well as other places. Christianity is having open doors it hasn't seen before. *Are we too tired to meet these trying times?* Like the disciples in Gethsemane, we are a tired people. This is true even though our cities have not been bombed, our production lines are humming, and our crops are abundant. We are tired from the years of war, our moral codes are weakening, and we are becoming more cynical. Yet in this very hour our church can triumph if we put forth an extra effort for Christ. It is possible to overcome our fatigue if we find something bigger than our fatigue to dedicate ourselves to. After Christ's resurrection, the tiredness of spirit of the disciples was overcome with the hope of the good news. Likewise, Paul kept his hope alive even in prison. It is the task of the church to light the candle of hope in these dark days. We have the motive; we have the way; and we have the hope for the world of tomorrow.

"The power of God" Mark 10:27. 3/10/46. "All things are possible with God." The power of God is more than we can conceive, but none of us draws on the power of God like we should. *Let us examine that power of God and understand better how we may have it for our life today.* We need to draw upon the power of God for the burdens that lie heavily on the human heart. We need to rely on Him for building the brotherhood of men. We need His power to help us overcome death and to assure our salvation. God makes all things new. *How can we obtain the power of God?* First, with God's help, we must empty our lives of selfish desires and seek His will. Second, we should determine to use God's power for noble purposes. Third, we must go to the Bible and study and pray to obtain His power. We need to empty ourselves so that God's power can flow through us.

"Do we care?" Luke 13:34. 3/24/46 (4/6/49, 8/19/54). Babies and small children are very self-centered. Most of us as adults are also self-centered in our relationship with God. We want Him to help us rather than wanting to serve Him. "What's in it for me?" we ask ourselves and we wonder if God really cares about us. Yes, the message of the Bible is that He cares for us deeply. But the question we are considering today is whether we care for Him. *In one sense, we don't seem to care.* We accept so many gifts of God, but we do so little in return for Him in gratitude. So few of us put God first in our lives, or put the work of the church before our other concerns. *In another sense, we do seem to care.* Yet underneath all of this indifference, I think we would really care if we seriously considered what God does for us in the gift of His Son. When people like Paul realized what God had done for them, they devoted their lives to His service and were willing to undergo severe persecution for His sake. Are we?

"The dignity of labor" Gen. 2:15. 9/1/46 (9/5/48). Labor Day is tomorrow to honor those who work whether it be with their heads or hands. God worked in creation and Adam worked tending the garden, and so work is counted as good. It is an eternal law that man must work or chaos will ensue. Paul said that within the Christian fellowship there was no place for the idler.

Our danger as a nation today is that too many people want something for free without work; that they want the government to take care of them, even though there are jobs available. *The Bible teaches the dignity of labor.* It does not matter so much the profession that we have, but that we all contribute as a carpenter, a fisherman, a tent maker, a landowner, a maker of dyes, etc. We have both the right and the responsibility to work. *Suggestions concerning the manner in which we dignify labor:* We need to view our labors as opportunities rather than as drudgeries. Some people have learned to find joy and dignity in their work, especially those doing creative work or producing useful products. When we can dedicate the work we do to something or someone greater than ourselves, we will also feel dignity in our work. The mother who cares for her child feels such dignity and fulfillment. God has made us co-laborers with Him in His world. God is not so concerned as to what job we have, but as to how well we do it. Whatever we do, we should bring glory to God so that we can hear His words to us, "Well done thou good and faithful servant."

"The Divine Union" John 17:21. 9/15/46 (6/6/48). The greatest failure of Christianity is not the hypocrisy that Christians are sometimes accused of, but the lack of vitality in the faith of so many "believers." In contrast, the greatest success of Christianity is in the lives of people whose faith sustains and empowers them and brings a glow to their lives. Today, my goal is to point out some steps we can take in the direction of union with the Divine. The purpose of Jesus' life was to draw men and women into this union with the Divine. This union is our one necessity and responsibility on earth. *Divine union means God for man and man for God.* We depend on and expect God to be for us. We pray for His help and for our salvation and depend on Him for our very life. Yet union means that we should also be givers. Jesus could sometimes not do miracles because of the lack of faith of people. God does not come into our lives unless we ask Him. We have to give and use our talents as our part in the union. God works in cooperation with man. We are partners with God and we depend on His power. We work in double yoke with Christ. As Paul says, "If God be for us, who can be against us?" We become lost in something bigger than ourselves. "For to me to live is Christ," Paul says. In other words our task is to pull ourselves together around the will and personality of God as seen in Christ. Until we integrate ourselves into something greater than ourselves, we will have no unity, no power, no peace, no security, or serenity of soul. Jesus said that "I am the Way." To find God, it must be through Him. He said also, "I and the Father are one. My supreme purpose in coming to earth was that you might be one in Us."

"Meeting life step by step" Matt. 6:34. 12/1/46 (3/10/47, 8/15/48, 8/22/48, 1/2/49, 1/11/53, 1/25/53, 6/12/55). (Revised several times). John Henry Newman in his hymn "Lead Kindly Light" writes, "I do not ask to see the distant scene. One step enough for me." He wrote it during a period of great anxiety for him in which he finally found peace. We too live in a time of great restlessness where we can't see far into the future. We need to learn to take life one step at a time. *Life can best be met, step by step.* Jesus also told his followers to "be not anxious for the morrow." We must make use of the present moment and not be overwhelmed by the size of the task before us or by the dimness of the future. This is a hard lesson for us, as instead of grasping the opportunities of the present, we want to look back at past successes and failures or to future goals. In football, we get to the final goal line in ten yard increments. What we do in the present is vitally important to the future. In the present, we face boredom and trifles as well as crises which may color the rest of our lives. To meet these crises without anxiety, we need God's help. The knowledge that an all wise God directs our lives, gives us courage and comfort. We may be inadequate, but God isn't. Many of our Presidents, including George Washington, Abraham Lincoln, and Woodrow Wilson, often sought God in their inadequacies and present failures, knowing that ultimate victory was God's. We must cast our sins and failures on Christ and take life step by step. We must go forward with Him, knowing that with Him leading us, final victory is ours in Him.

"The momentous message" John 10:10. 2/2/47 (6/15/49). The purpose of the church is to be a salesman for the universal church of Christ, for the kingdom of God. Yes, the church has made many mistakes and yes, there is sometimes no great longing for our spiritual merchandise. Yet we have a momentous message. Part of that message is that we know the way to abundant life. *This message is directed toward the individual.* Individuals today are mixed up and anxious about life because of the many problems that they don't know how to solve. The same was true in Jesus' day. The whole New Testament shows how Jesus gave new life, healing both physical and spiritual sickness. For those who were physically sick, he cured them; for those who were selfish, Christ showed that abundant life wasn't in material things, power, and honor, but in self-giving. *The message is directed towards society as a whole.* Changed individuals change society. The Christian message has led to momentous changes in society - in education, health care, prison reform, world peace and race relations. *The momentous message is about our new relationship with God.* The church's message to individuals and to the world tells us how to get right with God, to attune our lives to His principle of love, how to listen to His guidance, and how to work together with Him to achieve His ends. Submit to Him and let His spirit work within you and within society and life with all its fullness will be yours.

"Woman, behold thy son, behold thy mother" (Good Friday sermon) John 19:26-27. 3/26/48. In some homes, older parents are seen as burdens by their children. In Jesus' case, even while He is dying an excruciating death, He thinks of the welfare of His mother. In other passages in the Bible, Jesus makes clear that His primary duty was to His Father in heaven and He rebuked His family when they sought to interfere with this greater duty. This did not mean that He didn't love them, but that His task of ushering in the kingdom was bigger than they. Now, from the cross, He shows His love for His mother by making sure that she is taken care of by John, the disciple that He loved. John, the only disciple who had braved the angry mob, was given and accepted a great responsibility by his Lord. Tradition says that he stayed in Jerusalem for 12 years caring for Mary until her death.

"My God, my God, why hast thou forsaken me?" (Good Friday sermon) Matt. 27:46. 3/26/48. Man in his despair often cries out these words. But Christ's utterance of them cannot be compared in intensity. Our heart aches at the suffering we see and feel in the world and we ask "why, why?" Christ's suffering was so much greater than ours, however. We cannot imagine the physical agony of crucifixion that Jesus endured, but even worse was the spiritual pain of being condemned to death by a loving Father for the sins of the world. Was this a moment of weakness? Was Jesus quoting Psalm 22? We will never know, for the words are addressed not to us, but to God. We can only understand the meaning of the words by recalling that Jesus' purpose in the world was this moment, to sacrifice His life as the lamb of God for our sins. In the cross we see the terrible consequences of sin. Christ did not forsake God, for He said "my" God. Nor did God forsake Christ, as He gave Him victory over sin and death and raised Him to sit at His right hand. Let us show our gratitude for this tremendous sacrifice by a re-consecration of our lives to Him.

"Gaining personal religious experience" John 17:17. 10/10/48 (9/24/51, 7/1/52, 10/6/56, 8/10/58). "If anyone has the will to do God's will, he will know." Personal religious experience takes religion out of the realm of the theoretical to that of practical. It gives fire and meaning to religion. Many in religion have not had personal religious experiences, although many would love to have them. *An individual can only experience so many things.* There are some things that have to be accepted by faith. We accept the truth of the experiences of others every day because we trust their word even though we ourselves have never had the experience. We lean heavily on the experiences of others. We can work towards having the personal experience by placing ourselves in situations where those experiences are more possible. The same is true in Christianity. Only if we associate ourselves with the things of Christ can we hope to have a Christian religious experience. *We must work to rid our lives of those things that separate us from the Spirit of Christ.* Christ promises the vision of God to the pure of heart and not to the worldly wise. We have to lay aside our pet sins if we wish to see God. *We must persevere in seeking this goal of religious experience.* If we persevere, God honors our attempts. *Experience comes out of experiment.* We learn by living. Take the above steps and see if you don't begin to have deeper religious experiences. Try it.

"The fine art of appreciation" Luke 17:15-17. 11/21/48 (1/18/54). Only one of the ten people with leprosy cured by Christ came back to thank Him – a proportion that holds true today. The post office tells us that there are many letters written to Santa Claus asking for gifts, but very few thank you notes. *People want to feel appreciated.* William James said that "the deepest principle of human nature is the craving to be appreciated." We perform better when we are appreciated and encouraged than when we are criticized. This is a principle that is true in marriage, in business, and in public life. *There is a difference between appreciation and flattery.* Flattery is unkind because it is dishonest. Appreciation is thoughtful and sincere. People use flattery to win friends and influence people for their own advantage. *How can we develop true appreciation?* We can keep our eyes open to the wonders about us. "For the beauty of the earth, for the joy of human love, for all gentle thoughts and mild," as the hymn says. Open your eyes and you can see God working in the world and in your life. Open your eyes and see what others have done for you. So many have gone before us fighting for our freedoms, inventing useful products that we use, and making life safe and enjoyable for us. Our parents in particular have sacrificed much for our training and happiness. *We need to express our appreciation to them.* Our thanks must be real to us, but it is right and good that it be expressed. Let us be like the Samaritan who had leprosy and came back and praised God for His goodness. Let us not be like the nine who didn't.

"I want a job" Mark 5:18-19. 2/27/49. After having a great spiritual experience, people often clamor to God for a job. This is what the grateful man of the Gadarenes did to Jesus after he was cured. We say to God, "Here am I, send me." *Why then do we not offer ourselves to take up tasks in the church?* Some maybe feel they are not needed. Others let outside interests push aside the needs of the church. Still others do not feel that what they do for the church is really serving Christ. *Let us look at some things we can do for Christ's* *kingdom:* For example, every church has leadership positions that need to be filled. One should see these positions not as honorary positions, but as vital jobs that must be done. There is also the job of evangelism. All of us are called by Christ to spread the good news. Presbyterians do not do as good a job as many other denominations in this. We should be witnesses by our word and by our lives. The job of prayer is another one, as is witnessing in our homes. Using our money to further the interests of the kingdom of God is still another way of serving. Whatever our job is, organized or unorganized, personal or with others, there is a place that we can serve in the church. Like all jobs, there are certain qualifications required – sincerity of purpose, surrender of personality to God, a recognition of divine partnership, the realization that we need God's power, and finally the will to get started.

"Our reconciling God" 2 Cor. 5:19. 4/3/49 (4/19/49, 5/1/49, 8/28/49, 10/27/49, 3/21/51, 11/28/54). For some people, it is boring to talk about God because they have never fallen in love with Him as their loving, heavenly Father. We know of reconciliation within families, but today I want to talk about our reconciling God. *Certainly there is a need for reconciliation with God.* Individuals and nations today are far from God. We think that we will find happiness in sins, but we soon find that living in sin brings us no peace. God has taken the initiative to search for us and has reconciled us to Him through Christ. *We can stop that reconciling work of Christ* by letting selfishness and sin cancel what God has done for us. *God also uses human agents in His work of reconciliation.* We Christians serve as Christ's ambassadors by practicing reconciliation with others. As Christians we have the world's most marvelous message to preach, that God was in Christ reconciling the world unto Himself, not counting their trespasses against them.

"The faith we declare" Eph. 2:8-9. 10/30/49. Many members of our Protestant churches are unable to defend the faith they declare because they are unsure of just what it is. These then are some of the basic tenets of Protestantism: *Belief in God and Christ.* We believe in God as Creator and loving Father of Christians; that we owe Him love, loyalty, and obedience. We believe in a moral order and that Christ is God's Son whose sacrifice on the cross was to restore broken harmony between God and mankind and lead us out of our sinful ways. *Belief in the Church universal.* We believe in an invisible universal spiritual Church whose head is the living Christ and not a human representative. We work through visible churches, but we do not think that they are infallible. *Justification by faith rather than works.* We are not saved by any visible church or the forgiveness declared by men. Nor are we saved by works that we do or pay for. We are saved by our trustful faith in Christ.

Good works are an outgrowth of our faith and not the means to our salvation. *Priesthood of the believers.* Every believer in Christ has access to God, and no other intermediary - such as a priest - is necessary. Christ is our only mediator. *Separation of Church and State.* In our day, communism declares the power of the state over the church and Roman Catholicism declares the power of the church over the state. Protestantism believes in freedom of religion. *Authority of the Bible.* We believe that doctrines should be based on Biblical proof and not on tradition or the decisions of councils. The Bible has a central place in Protestant churches. Through the Bible we will know the truth, and the truth will make us free. We have a glorious faith that we should take care to not lose because of indifference or ignorance.

"The church makes religious news" 1/15/50. This is a Sunday evening "sermon." *World news about the church:* The ecumenical movement is in the news. This is a movement towards cooperation, and in some cases unity, between the different denominations in different countries. Particular attention is given to the difficulties of the church in communist countries and of the tensions between Protestants and Catholics in some Catholic countries. *The national scene:* There are efforts going on to unite different Protestant groups including all Presbyterian bodies. In Mobile, there are attempts to bring together Christians to meet urban needs. Differing views of what the separation of church and state means to different churches are discussed with such cases as hymn singing in public schools, the distribution of Bibles by the Gideons, and funding for Catholic schools mentioned. The Baptists, in particular, are pushing efforts to keep the separation of church and state intact. *News concerning the Presbyterian Church in the US:* News is given about general assemblies and reorganization of the PCUS and about Government Street Presbyterian Church, including its building program. *Odds and ends:* News is mentioned about the high costs of funerals, advertising efforts to get more people to come to church, free trips to church being offered by bus and taxi companies, the use of free parking space on Sunday, and of retired bankers and policemen becoming ministers.

"The marks of a great church" Acts 1:14. 2/26/50 (4/15/51, 6/3/51, 2/5/53, 2/20/53, 3/8/53, 8/24/58). What makes a great church beyond architecture and location? Here are a few ideas: *The mark of a great church is a church marked by prayer.* We must have personal, private, and public prayer. A deep prayer life is fundamental as our scripture points out in Acts. "These all continued with one accord in prayer and supplication." It is through prayer that worship is created. We must pray to understand God. *The mark of a great church is a high mark of purpose.* The purpose of the church should be more than just to hear a speaker, to have a sanctuary from troubles, or to perpetuate family relationships. The purpose of the church is to evangelize, to be a colony of heaven on earth, the advance guard of the kingdom of God. This is done by individuals accepting their responsibility to fulfill the command of Christ. *The mark of a great church is its willingness to sacrifice.* The blood of martyrs was the seed of the early church. How ready are we to make sacrifices today? *The mark of a great church is its willingness to serve.* Jesus says that the greatest among us are those who serve others. Our church serves others in its benevolence budget and in its mission work, both here at home and abroad. Sometimes it is easier to give money than time. The church serves also when it stirs our moral conscience to action, not only about individual sins, but also about social sins. *The mark of a great church is to be spirit filled.* This is what distinguishes it from man-made organizations – the conviction that we are called by God for our work.

"Meeting life's dangers" Eph. 6:12. 7/16/50. There are many dangers facing us in life. *There is the danger that we will become cold and indifferent about life.* Life is full of wonders and the child is filled with awe. A danger is that we lose that child's awe and become bored, cynical, and indifferent and lose our youthful idealism. *Second, there is the danger of life becoming sordid.* Our indifference to the good and the beautiful lead us to that which is sordid and unrefined. When we abuse the good things of life, they become sordid. For example, too much social drinking can lead to alcoholism. *Third, there is the danger of limiting your life's usefulness.* Too many think of life only in terms of making money. We need financial security, but we need also to use our talents to help others and do God's will. We all have ways that we can be useful to others. Maybe the dangers you face are different, but whatever they are, you can face them being clothed in God's armor. This armor consists of truth, faith, and the hope of salvation. We can be filled with the Spirit of Christ and learn to overcome the dangers that face us and to live life fully.

"The value of an idea" Mark 1:13-14. 9/1/50. In Germany, the idea of one man brought the world to a world war. Today, the ideas of communism and of democracy and free enterprise clash. In science, the wonder of ideas has given birth to marvelous changes in our material world. Religious ideas are also powerful forces. Many times people mock at new ideas, but then later, these ideas conquer. Ideas have great power for good and for evil. The Christian idea is the most powerful of all ideas because even evil cannot stand up to it. Millions have been transformed by it. We need to put the idea of Christianity to work in our lives. Jesus not only presented the idea of the kingdom of God, He personified that idea in His own life. He showed us the idea of "God the

Father" in His actions. When our ideas are transformed from the abstract to the practical, they become powerful. *We must let idealism control our ideas.* We need not only to personify our ideas, but to put them under the control of our highest ideals. With idealism we have power and purpose.

"Magnificent possession" I Cor. 6:19-20. 1/27/51 (3/18/56). Much emphasis today is placed on what we possess. We think our happiness is in what we own, but we are wrong. Our happiness is in what possesses us. *At times possession brings tragedy.* When evil takes over, sometimes we say, "I don't know what possessed me." In New Testament times, people were possessed by demons, while today, people are possessed by the greed for riches, power, or pleasure. *People can also be possessed by good forces.* Sometimes ideals and positive dreams control people and these persons end up doing a lot of good for mankind. Paul says that we can be so possessed by the Spirit of God that we become the temple of God. *What being possessed by Christ means.* It means that Christ can use each of us, no matter how humble we are, to make something beautiful out of life. A famous violinist said that the music is not in the instrument, rather it is in the one who plays it. We are transformed into useful tools by the Spirit of Christ to help bring in the kingdom. Louis Pasteur gave credit to Christ for what he accomplished. Life becomes enriched when we are possessed by God's Spirit. Marriages that have Christ at the center are abundant marriages. We Christians are no longer our own because Christ died for us. Paul expresses this when he says "It is no longer I that live, but Christ lives in me." Our chief end as Christians is to glorify God and to enjoy Him forever. All else - our vocations, our hopes, our ambitions, and our actions - are governed by our loyalty to God. We are not our own, and it is in God's possession of us that we find triumphant living. God matters more than anything else.

"Repetitious religion" Deut. 6:3-9. 2/11/51 (8/25/51, 5/18/58). People often complain that they hear the same thing from ministers year in and year out. Religion, however, must be repetitious, like the mother insisting that the child wash his hands and eat his vegetables. One dose is not enough. Some types of repetition, however, are undesirable, such as when religion becomes just a form without substance. This type of repetition receives condemnation in the Bible. Liturgy is meant to guide, but it too can lose its beauty and become a dead form if our minds and hearts are not involved. Some hymns have words that would be untrue if we sung them. Sometimes we repeat the creed and the Lord's Prayer just as words without meaning. This is impure repetition. Presbyterians believe in sanctification, the work of God's free grace whereby we are renewed and enabled to die more and more to sin and to live unto righteousness. Our worship should help us grow in righteousness, and if it doesn't, it is formalism and false worship. God wants our worship to be true. *There is a form of repetitious religion that is vital and for which we ought to rejoice.* If we have found joy in our religion, then we need to repeat it to others. God tells Israel to always keep before them what God has done for them as a people. He has revealed Himself to them and delivered them. They were to put God's law on their foreheads and stamp it on their doorposts and teach it to their children. *Some things we ought never to tire of repeating or hearing.* For example, that man is a sinner, as all have fallen short of the glory of God; there is no other name under heaven, given among men, whereby we must be saved, except the name of Jesus Christ; that man is saved by Christ's grace and our acceptance of it; and that if we are children of God, why should we fear?

"God in the affairs of men" Heb. 2:1-9. 11/4/51. We can concentrate on Christianity's failures or its successes in the last 2,000 years. As for its failures, it has failed to prevent wars or to create universal brotherhood and good will. We are going to concentrate, however, on the successes. I truly believe that God has placed everything in subjection to Christ, but His and our work is not yet done. The influence of Christ has reached into every part of our society. *Christianity has not conquered all, but it has influenced all.* Frightful forces are arrayed against it, including much in the human heart. Yet Christianity continues advancing throughout the world. The position of women has improved, humanitarian work has spread, and through Christian leaders peace and unity are advanced. We see the effects of Christianity in our consciences, in politics, business, service clubs, and science. Among many other things, Christianity awakens in us the need for fair play, honesty, and stability of character. It awakens us to what is wrong and to the need to correct it. Through Christianity, those who are troubled by fears and sorrows, find peace and hope; those whose sin is weighty, find relief.

"The impact of Christ upon the world" Luke 1:49-53. (Christmas sermon) 12/23/51. This is Christ's day and in our celebrations we should make Him central. The impact of Christ has changed the world. *Impact of Christ is felt through His life:* Christ has called not only His disciples, but people through all the centuries, including us, to follow Him. And as people have done that, their lives have been changed, and through them , the world has changed. So many of the great advances in the world can be traced back to the changed lives of Christians who have been influenced by the example of Christ as a healer and one who cares for the poor and outcasts. *Impact of Christ in His teachings:* It was Christ's teachings that showed men how to live, gave meaning to life, and put material and spiritual things in their proper place. It was His teaching that revealed God to man and the importance of the individual to God. He gave life a new value. He put purpose into all that we do. He took away our fear of death and replaced it with hope. He took away our sins and redeemed us. "Thou shalt call His name Jesus for He shall save His people from their sins." But today, He needs committed Christians who have given themselves wholeheartedly to Him to make an impact on the world. But how can the world be changed through us if others see in us people who are fearful, greedy, lack the spirit of brotherhood, or who seek only the things of the world? Just as Jesus depended on His disciples to carry the gospel to the world, He depends on us. Let's be true to that trust.

"Wither?" John 14:4-5. 6/1/52. (Nursing school) (6/30/52). Like Thomas, many of us do not know where we are going in this life. Yet we need to think about our personal goals even though we may feel that we will not be able to have a great effect on society. Either by chance or by choice we determine the direction of our lives. Some leave their lives to chance, but doing so is very dangerous. Others try to make decisions. Christ made his decision at age 12. "I must be about my Father's business." He chose to head towards the cross. You in this graduating class have already chosen your profession, but you must also choose a direction for your lives. *Guideposts on the way:* Gain a consciousness of God's partnership in your life. Whittier in a poem says that "To one fixed trust my spirit clings; I know that God is good!" God's love, purpose, and presence was Whittier's "whither." Life held no fear for him. Secondly, for life to have meaning, it must be filled with a desire to serve. Great doctors and nurses are not ones thinking always of money, but those who think of service. "Quo vadis?" I go the way of Christ, the way of truth and life.

"So you want to be a disciple?" John 15:8. 2/24/52. Most of us want to be onlookers, followers, and listeners, but not disciples of Jesus Christ. Discipleship is too costly. *A disciple must be a person who will grow like his master.* Christ pulled out only a few special followers from the fickle masses to train them as to His purpose, and use them as His witnesses. Sometimes they were slow to understand Him and His teachings. Today, we as Presbyterians believe in the Westminister Confession, but that doesn't make us into automatic disciples of Christ. Discipleship means growth as well as orthodoxy. Peter grew in his understanding of God's ways and so must we. For example, we have grown in our understanding about things like slavery and race relations, and a hundred years from now, we may have matured even more. Discipleship means not only a growth in understanding, but also in love. *A* *disciple must be boldly adventurous.* Jesus constantly said "Be not afraid." Yet, most of the disciples died violent deaths for their Master. They risked their lives daily to spread His message. Today, we don't necessarily need to risk our lives, but we should be willing to risk our reputations and wealth as disciples of Jesus. There is nothing easy about the Christian religion. *A disciple must be guided by a great faith.* Our work as Christians is guided by our faith that God will honor our small efforts to follow Him. *A disciple must have a surrendered life.* Discipleship means the denial of self and surrender to Christ and to His purposes. We need to use our work, time, and talents for Him. *A disciple must bear fruit.* Can people see in our lives fruit that makes them want to be a disciple as well – a full, abundant, and joyful life? Every sermon should be preached for a decision, and I hope that your decision today is to become a disciple of Christ, to participate actively in bringing in His kingdom.

"News not views" Romans 10:15. 6/8/52. In Mobile Bay, an unusual phenomenon occurs from time to time when crabs and fish by the thousands wash up to shore. The cry, "Jubilee," goes out and people come running to the beach to collect in buckets and baskets the bounty from the sea. When the cry goes out, it is time to act and not to philosophize. The New Testament is mostly about news and not views – the good news of the saving work of Jesus and of His resurrection. Even today, the news of our salvation is still fresh. Other news grows stale and old, but not the good news of the Gospel. *All manner of news:* There is a message for all the ages and races and sexes and circumstances in the New Testament. It was proclaimed to all of us who are entrapped by evil or in despair. *Christian news announced in various ways:* The transforming news of the kingdom of God is announced in various ways. Sometimes it is preached in terms of the needs of the individual, sometimes in terms of the social gospel. Just as God calls us to transform individuals, God also calls us to transform institutions and society and to eternal fellowship with Him. *How can it be called good news since it demands sacrifice?* Christ tells us that we must lose our lives for Him and warns us of the hardships that we will face. But the good news is that God cares about us deeply, that He is reconciling the world to Himself, that He believes in us, loves us, and forgives us as individuals. That is the good news and our hope. It is good news also because His way of sacrifice is the way of abundant living. It is the most powerful news in the world. Imagine what society would look like if we had never received this good news. So many works and organizations of good will have been based on this news. So many lives captivated by evil and selfishness, have been set free because of it. *Why then do not more take advantage of it?* Some of us still don't believe that it is possible. Others of us see Christians who say one thing and do another and so aren't convinced. Today, let us accept the good news of salvation and then spread it to others by our words and by our lives. "How pleasant is the coming of those with glad good news."

"Watch your judgment" 6/22/52 (3/23/57). When Jesus said "judge not" he meant censorious judgment and quick condemnation without looking at the facts. He meant that we must avoid detraction and slander. We are not talking about God's judgment, which is a future certainty, nor are we talking about intellectual and ethical appraisals. *How easy it is to judge others.* We like juicy news about people we don't like, or about causes that we are prejudiced against, and so we bear false witness to others, not taking time to check out the facts. *Why then does Christ emphasize that we ought to avoid this mistake?* For one thing, motives are difficult to judge. For another, we know only half the truth. *Who are we to judge?* We are all mixed bags of good and evil. The way that we judge others, we ourselves will be judged. We may judge others of sexual sins, avarice, and false ambition, and yet we ourselves have those same tendencies. *If you must judge, judge yourself.* If we are tempted to pass judgment on others, let us first ask ourselves what we would have done in similar circumstances. Let us judge our own actions and where we have failed God, remembering that God who knows all about us, will use with us the same standard that we use with others.

"Standing up to life" Acts 2:14. 10/26/52. In facing what to do with life, we have three choices: We can run away from life in drugs or alcohol or suicide. We can drift with life, running along with it, taking the line of least resistance. Or we can stand up to life, facing it and using it for good ends. This is what Peter did in the text. "Peter, standing up with the eleven, lifted up his voice and said to them." After this verse, Peter preaches his Pentecost sermon that swayed a multitude. He stood up to opposition and convinced them. *He could do it because he had a message.* Peter believed in Christ and in His resurrection with all of his heart. He had to proclaim it because it was true. *He could do it because he had encouragement from others.* Peter failed often, but this day, he was standing with the other eleven disciples and received from them added strength. *He could do it because he had the sense of God's power working in him.* Peter had just experienced the coming of the Holy Spirit. We today also have the message of life, if we take our religion seriously. But to really know Christianity, we have to live it, to have experienced its power and peace. Today, we also need the encouragement of others who have gone before us and those with us now as we walk and proclaim the Christian life. It is discouraging for a minister who takes a moral stand in his community to find that his congregation is not with him. Most importantly, we need the sense of God's presence and power if we are to stand up to life. "If God is for us, who can be against us?" As Moody said, "Let God have your life, He can do more with it than you can." Life is not easy, but we were not made in God's image in order to run away from it.

"How to listen to a sermon" Matt 7:24. 12/7/52 (1/4/53, 2/16/53, 3/14/55, 5/22/55, 10/16/55, 1/22/56, 5/6/57, 6/17/57). When Christ preached, some "heard him gladly," others were "offended" or "amazed" or "sad." When Paul preached, one person fell asleep and fell out of a window. We need instructions for attending a football game, and we need instructions for listening to a sermon. *The first requirement for any good sermon listener is to prepare yourself.* We need to prepare our minds and hearts by raising them from our daily concerns to God. The hymns, the scriptures, and the prayers help prepare our minds. Many times, the subject matter of the sermon may not be what you are needing at the moment, but listen anyway, and put it away for another time as a kind of spiritual storehouse. *Secondly, apply the sermon to your personal life.* Use your imagination and incorporate the message into your life. *Thirdly, consecrate your life to God.* "Be not hearers, but doers." The preacher is not there to entertain you. He is there to challenge you to live a life closer to God. He is doing the best that he can, but he depends on you. Hear him, heed him, and then help him.

"The possible you" I John 3:2. 7/19/53. Most of us want to change our lives into something better. God sees the possible you. *Some people can see below the surface to the possible you.* Jesus knew what was in man for evil and for good. He transformed rough fishermen and publicans into disciples. He saw the good in sinners of all types and in little children. This ability to have a vision of transformed reality is a wonderful gift. It happened in this nation when our forefathers recognized "the possible you" in all the rough characters who had settled it. *It is important that we see "the possible you" in ourselves and work towards it.* We have so many possibilities and we should use these in the service of our Lord.

"Meeting life's perplexities" Exodus 14:11-15. 11/15/53. The sign of our times is the question mark. We all face perplexities that weigh heavily on us. Nationally, we face the problem of peace, crime waves, the cost of living, political scandals, and communism. Individually, we face moral problems, marriage problems, children perplexities, economic problems, and the problems of living a Christian life in an unchristian society. How should we meet these problems? In the case of Israel facing the barrier of the Red Sea, the people said, "give up and go back;" Moses said, "stand still;" and God said 'go forward!" *The people said, give up and go back.* This is the easiest way as it means returning to the familiar, even though in the case of Israel, it was a life of misery in slavery. The people attacked Moses and wallowed in self-pity and that sapped their courage. Like Job's wife, they said, "curse God and die." *Moses said, stand still and see the salvation of the Lord.* This is another way of facing perplexities. Moses wanted the people to pause and think through their decision -- to see where they were and how they got there and the meaning of it all. Stand firm. *God said, go forward and conquer.* Dare to do the impossible, even crossing through the sea, because of your faith that God is with you. Jesus tells His disciples to launch out into the deep as fishermen, and after His death and resurrection, to go forward into the world and conquer. Troubles produce endurance, endurance character, and character hope. We triumph in our troubles as we go forward in our faith.

"How can I serve?" Acts 9:6. 2/20/54. In Biblical stories, usually a grateful person asks this question after a tremendous experience of deliverance from sin or distress. While the natural man asks, "What's in it for me?" the spiritual person asks, "How can I serve?" His sense of responsibility has been stirred. Some ask the question without first considering the cost, like the rich young ruler who found out that the cost of following Jesus was more than he was willing to pay. Others, though, are willing to make the sacrifices involved. *How best can you serve God?* You serve God mainly by the kind of person you are. The real hope of the church is people controlled by God's Spirit. Some may not have great financial resources, but their very life is an inspiration and service to others. We can serve God by prayer. This is a service even shut-ins can do. If our prayers are to be effective we need, however, to pray with un-prejudiced and unselfish hearts. We can also serve by speaking a good word for Christ in our contacts with others. I yearn that this church, so full of history, wealth, and talented individuals, will have an effect on this community. But first, there has to be the spirit in its members of wanting to serve.

"The Christian extra" Matt. 5:46. 5/2/54. "What do ye more than others." We must be willing to work for those things that we say we believe in. Christianity takes the normal way of living and gives it something extra to make it into abundant living. *This Christian power is not found in usual channels.* Too often we Christians judge ourselves by worldly standards of success, such as money and social prestige. The rabbis of Jesus' time judged according to the laws that were followed or broken. Many of us judge ourselves by man's standards rather than by God's standards. We are satisfied in being nominal Christians and don't want to give the extra needed. *Jesus taught us in His ministry what that extra was.* It was going the extra mile, the extra turning of the cheek, love for enemies, forgiving seventy times seven. Jesus showed us the extra by loving us while we were sinners. We are told by Jesus to be perfect. We fear that we will never attain it in this life, but we are still called to work towards it. We are the examples that others have of what a Christian life should be, so we should live it as best we can. Such a life will bring up the level of the society around us, as the power of Christ in our lives is a revolutionary force.

"The security of the Christian faith" Psalm 16:8. 5/9/54. Everyone desires a sense of security. "Security" is a relative term, sometimes meaning a job and source of income, a nest egg in the bank, insurance, a home, health, the love of someone, or a happy family. We sometimes get ulcers as we struggle for security. Our nation spends millions in military preparation and in signing pacts hoping for security. *The Bible is explicit in teaching that there can be no security where sin reigns, or where a life is under captivity to sin.* The stories of so many persons like Adam and Eve, Saul, David, and Judas confirm this. Even though we live in king's palaces, if we live in sin, we have no peace and no security. *Again, the Bible is clear in revealing that any security based on trust in other gods, but the true one is only fancied security, which cannot stand the tests of life.* We don't worship wooden or metal idols today, but we do worship things like money and possessions. There is no stability in material things. There is also the false god of self which fails us. *What is the Biblical source of security?* Those who seek to lead a righteous life under God's direction find peace amidst the storms. Security comes from trust in God, letting Him take control of our lives. The Lord is our shield and our rock. We know that God is good and wishes our good. "If God be for us, who can be against us?" Having this kind of confidence and trust, Christians live secure while the world tumbles down around them. Have you found this secret for yourself, my friend?

"The strength found in afflictions" Acts 14:22, 2 Cor. 4:17. 5/16/54. Good can come out of evil, even though it is hard to believe when we are in the midst of the evil. *What the word affliction connotes to us today.* To be afflicted means "to be struck down." Some are struck with failures and disappointments, broken dreams, and unfulfilled desires. Others are hit by sickness and disabilities, or with problems greater than they can solve. Affliction can be mental, physical, or social. *Afflictions can lead to failure and despair.* They can lead to alcohol and to suicide. *The strength that can be found in our afflictions.* Afflictions can bring us to God and His kingdom, as broken hearts become open hearts. We come to realize that we need outside strength and we learn to trust in a Higher Power, which gives us that strength. *But afflictions also work to release God-given powers within our life.* Great problems in a nation's life often bring out the best in us and in our leaders. Social problems bring out the best in reformers like Wilberforce and Booth. Affliction may be the very thing that will bring strength and beauty to our character. *You must be ready for afflictions.* We prepare for afflictions by building up a reservoir of faith and trust, through reading the Bible and through worship. When we need the reservoir, it is there.

"Don't vacate your faith on your vacation" Mark 6:31. 6/13/54. So much of our activity is directionless. The disciples were tired and weary when Jesus said to them to come apart into a desert place and rest awhile. While they were with Him resting, He gave them words of life. *More and more people have vacations.* There are scheduled times in the week and the year when we have time off to ourselves, and we should learn to use this time well. Leisure time has increased greatly because of increased productivity. It's not so much where we go, but what we do, that determines the success or failure of a vacation. *How do you spend your vacation time?* Some use it to do as they please, even if it means immorality. Most of us, though, want to spend our time well for physical and spiritual re-creation. It is a time for change for our bodies and our minds. It is also a time to be still and know God. It is a time to come face to face with self, to reappraise our work and our purpose for living. Are we the persons we were meant to be? Are we in tune with God and His will? When you go on vacation in the mountains or over the bay or just at home, don't forget to take your faith with you and to strengthen it.

"Do we mean business when we say, "we care?" Luke 9:62. 8/19/54. Our text is about the man who desired to follow Jesus, but came up with excuses about when he would do it. Are we really serious in our desire to follow Jesus? *We certainly mean business when we ask if God cares.* Is God really interested in us as individuals? Is the universe friendly? If God doesn't care, then all is lost. God has shown that He means business when He says that He cares for man. The whole story of the Bible is about how much God cares and it culminates in the sacrifice of Jesus Christ and in His resurrection. God cares for sure, but do we care? *We show by our convictions whether we mean business when we say we care.* The disciples, the reformers, and missionaries had strong convictions about the truth of the Gospel and were willing to suffer for Christ. Today, we, too, need such convictions. *By our charity, we reveal whether we mean business when we say we care.* How much time and money do we give to benevolent causes to help others and not just to help ourselves? How we use our money is often the acid test of our heart's desire. *By our conduct we reveal whether we mean business when we say we care.* Words are cheap, but the test of conduct is the hardest of all. Jesus said that "by their fruits you shall know them." Our actions show the world how serious we are about our faith. It was the conduct of Christians, and not the message of Christians, that turned Ghandi against the Christian church. *By our consciousness of our commission we reveal to the world that we mean business when we say we care.* The great commission of Christ was for us to go into all the world, the world of our business and social relationships, and tell others of the good news of Christianity. We are a colony of heaven on earth. We are in partnership with God to help bring in the kingdom. Do we really have a sense of this partnership and purpose for our lives? I believe that we as a church care, but let's be reminded of the great work that is before us. And then let us do it.

"Forward with Christ" Mark 16:20. 9/5/54. This will be the spiritual theme of the Presbyterian Church U.S. for the next three years. But before going forward with Christ, people need to return to Christ because many have thrust religion aside. They feel that is has no place in the modern mind. How then are we to fulfill our task as followers of Christ? *The early apostles went forward under the direction of prayer.* It is in prayer that the apostles, and we today, receive our directions from Christ. Prayer was an essential part of the lives of the disciples and of the early church. It is the essential element for the national revivals of the past and for going forward today. *They went forward with a purpose.* They wanted to evangelize the world as Christ had told them to do – to let everyone know the good news of his resurrection and of man's reconciliation with God. That is still our mission today. Besides evangelism, going forward means offering service to people in need. It also means preaching prophetically to call people's attention to the sins and ills in our societies and in ourselves. *They went forth with divine power.* Jesus went with His disciples in Spirit for He said, "Lo, I am with you always." As the text says, "The Lord working with them." This type of going forward with Christ sometimes requires the sacrifice by us of family, of possessions, and even of life. Let us go forward to our Christian world task in that spirit.

"The minister looks at the layman's ministry" John 17:6-18. 11/28/54. As the minister looks at the layman's ministry he sees two things: *First, he sees the tremendous temptations that face laypersons in their ministry.* One temptation is for them to say that they pay the staff to run the church and that's what they should do. But that way, laypersons miss the joy of volunteer service and fail to grow spiritually themselves. A second temptation is laziness. Laypersons want to be involved, but never quite get around to it. A third temptation is that they feel unworthy. Yet we all have talents and those talents should be used for the glory of God and service to others. A fourth temptation is that they are afraid of the opinion of others. They fear being laughed at as being too religious, of being too goody-goody. *Secondly, the minister sees the many opportunities that await the Christian layperson.* There is the opportunity of participating in church organization as elders, deacons, and ushers. There is the opportunity of personal evangelism in the social and business life. There is the opportunity to make religion a week-day fact in life. Without you laypersons, the minister is helpless. You are the ones who take the preaching, as poor as it is, into the world. The church is yours. You are the church. Your financial pledge is one thing, but your life is the most important thing to dedicate to Christ through this church.

"Nevertheless" Luke 22:42. 12/5/54. The word "nevertheless" can signify a tremendous change in a person's life, like the turntable that turns a locomotive around. *Nevertheless as it affects our acceptance of our Christian task.* "Father, if Thou be willing, remove this cup from me; nevertheless, not my will but thine be done." Jesus was facing the horrors and suffering of humiliation and death on the cross in the most painful way imaginable, as well as the hell of separation from His Father. Nevertheless, He set His face towards the plan of God. Paul says "For me to live is Christ and to die is gain, nevertheless to abide in the flesh is more needful for you." Thank God for church people today who, while they know it is easier to belong to the 'church of the heavenly rest,' put their shoulder to the wheel and do the work that is required of them for the good of the kingdom of God. *Nevertheless as it affects our acceptance of life.* In the 73rd Psalm, the psalmist looks at life and sees how the evil have prospered and seemingly are not plagued like the righteous. But he says, "nevertheless I am continually with you; you hold me by my right hand." When we face trouble and want to give up, that word "nevertheless" strengthens us and assures us of God's love and power. As the psalmist sums it up for us in the 31st Psalm, "I said in haste, I am cut off from before thine eyes: Nevertheless thou heardest the voice of my supplications when I cried unto thee."

"Christ born in you" Col 1:27. 12/19/54 (Christmas sermon). If Christ is born only in Bethlehem but not in us, it does us little good. Paul constantly mentions the necessity of having Christ live in us, such as, "Christ in you the hope of glory," and, "if any man be in Christ he is a new creature." We shouldn't worry so much about there being no room in the inn, but about whether there is room in our hearts for Him. What does it mean to have Christ born in us? *Christ in us means a man draws his sustenance from God in Christ.* A Christian has a new source of power in his life that lets him face troubles with serenity. The power behind the universe is on our side. *Christ in us means that we endeavor to live a God-centered existence.* We need to ask ourselves each day, 'who is going to be God today, me or God?' "We must let go and let God." *Christ in us means new unity.* Paul says "For ye are all one in Christ." If we have Christ in our hearts, we will be brothers and sisters with all peoples. *Christ in us means a new being.* C.S. Lewis says "God became man to turn creatures into sons—not simply to produce better men." How then can the Spirit of Christ be born in us? It is not by being good, and not by knowledge, but a work of grace on God's part. The key is our acceptance of the fact by faith - either sudden faith, or the result of many years of struggle and growth. We know that we have that faith by the fruit of our spiritual life – love, joy, hope, longsuffering. The finest way we can celebrate Christmas is to give our hearts to God so that the Spirit of Christ can reign within us.

"Judgment is now, too" Matt. 3:10. 3/7/55 (8/28/55, 10/18/55, 5/9/57) Judgment comes not just when our lives are covered with evil, but also when our spiritual life begins to disintegrate. There are two distinct uses of the term judgment: There is the judgment of the future, the last judgment, when we will all stand before the throne of God. But there is also the judgment of now. "The wages of sin is death," Paul says, not "will be" death. Judgment comes in our daily decisions that determine the direction and character of our future lives. Our activities are judgment and we will reap what we have sown. If we abuse our bodies, we will inherit the results of that abuse. Cheating a little today can lead to the destruction of character and terrible loss later. Judgment can also come in the form of a hurting conscience. Sin brings judgment later, but also now. *Is there anything that we can do?* Some of us feel sin to be a burden too heavy for us to bear. There is nothing we can do, for Christ has done it for us. That is the message of Christianity and why it is called the "good news." We have forgiveness for our sins through Christ. Paul says, "the wages of sin is death, but the gift of God is eternal life through Jesus Christ our Lord." The road to peace with God is through Jesus Christ. Judgment is a time of condemnation, but it is also a time when God shows His great mercy to us.

"Paul's answer to a king" Acts 26:28-29. 4/17/55. Paul was before Agrippa witnessing to the good news of Christ and Agrippa said to Paul, "In a short time you think to make me a Christian." And Paul said, "whether short or long, I would to God that not only you, but also all who hear me this day might become such as I am – except these chains." Others have preached before kings, rulers, and sultans including St. Francis and John Knox. Paul's answer shows the strength and joy of the Christian faith as it comes face to face with the powers of the world. Paul was not fearful of the king or envious of him, but instead wanted to share what he had with him. What did Paul want to share with the king? *Paul wanted Agrippa to have a faith in the purposes of God.* Kings come and go, but the purposes of God remain. So Paul wanted for the Jewish Agrippa a life steadied by the knowledge of God's purpose in the world, the redemption of mankind through Christ. If our individual purpose is tied to God's overall purpose, then we are indeed fortunate. *Paul wanted Agrippa to have faith in the resurrection and experience the power of the resurrection.* While Agrippa had Rome on his side, Paul had God on his. *Paul wished that King Agrippa could have the experience of the heavenly vision which had been Paul's.* That vision brought him joy. In summary, Paul tells Agrippa, I don't envy you your power because I know the fears it brings with it. Instead, I wish you could have the purpose in life and the joy that I have, knowing the good news and power of the resurrected Christ.

"Christ's man" Romans 8:9. 5/22/55. Who is Christ's man or woman? The 12 disciples were strong in their individuality and none of them were perfect. *Christ's person is an individual bought with a price.* We must realize the extreme sacrifice of what Christ has done for us. *Christ's person is a person who lets Christ be the Lord of their life.* When we turn our thoughts to being God's person instead of our own, we become Christ's person. *Christ's person is a person filled with the Spirit of Christ.* Our life will then bear the fruit of this Spirit. *Christ's person, while not being perfect, is striving for perfection.* Like Paul, we "press on" to higher and higher goals. *Christ's person is one who does His commandments.* Paul was called to do a task, to fulfill the purpose Christ had for him. Christ wants us to be His person by beginning where we are. As Douglas Steere says, "we were sent to be spent." We cannot be Christ's and not be willing to work." Christ wants us to be His men and women. We need to put Him and not other things first in our lives. We can't keep putting off the choice. Today, won't you become Christ's man or Christ's woman?

"The higher command" Acts 22:14-16. 6/5/55 (6/26/55). In schools across the nation, thousands have graduated and are now thinking about their life's work. But all of us should be thinking about our life's work, even if we aren't graduating. All of us Christians are under a higher command, the command of God, for higher service. Not just ministers and missionaries are under orders, but we are all under orders. "Every man's life is a plan of God." God chose us for our particular task, and so we need to go out and bear fruit. *Paul recognized that he was called by God.* The God of his fathers had chosen him to have a part in working out God's eternal plan. All of us progress because we stand on the shoulders of those who have gone before us. *Paul was called for a purpose.* He was called to be a witness to all men of the glory of Jesus. We witness as much by our lives as by our words. *Paul had to prepare himself to fulfill God's purpose.* He had to learn God's will through prayer, through his mind, through discernment, and through practice. He had to keep his eye on Christ just as we have to do today in 1955. *Paul was urged to be up and* *working.* Too many of us learn God's will, but we do not put it into practice. "And now, why tarriest thou?" The spreading of God's kingdom depends on you because you can go where a minister cannot reach.

"One step at a time" Matt. 6:34. 6/12/55. Life is so ordained that we meet its challenges day by day, one step at a time. This is the way that those who have been ill learn to walk again. *If the burdens all came at once, it would be more than we could bear.* Many of us think about our problems all at once – past, present, and future. *It is tragic when we do this.* If we approach life in this way, we will be overwhelmed. If we provide our children with all the material things that they need when they first marry, they don't have the joy of building a life and a home together, piece by piece, one step at a time. The experience of success and failure in small doses makes us stronger. *We need a growing faith.* The disciples' faith in Christ gradually grew. First they saw Him as a man, then a prophet, then the Messiah, and then the Son of God whose Spirit was still with them even after His death. Our faith, too, needs to grow. We start where we are, and if we have open minds and hearts, we will grow step by step. The power of the Holy Spirit will lead us into all truth. *We can grow into usefulness in the service of Christ.* We can do small tasks or give small amounts and see if God will lead us to give more and do more. *In the Christian life we have One who leads us step by step.* We are not left to our own courage and wisdom. We have the security of knowing that God who loves us, is by our side leading us. The step of yesterday is past. All we have is the step of today.

"When a man comes to himself" Luke 15:17-18. 9/18/55. When the prodigal son found himself, he turned his back on his miserable life and returned home to his loving Father. In 1955, we probably don't see ourselves as the prodigal for business is booming, the stock market is up, and more homes are being built. Yet, we need to come to our true selves by recognizing our self in relationship to God's plan for us. *We will fulfill our place only when we come to ourselves.* When we see our opportunities, our duties, and our purpose in life, we come to ourselves. Without this awareness, we won't be able to live the abundant life that Christianity promises. We need to find our life's work, and when we do, we are filled with joy. We need to realize that we are children of God. Surrounding us are spiritual powers that will feed our souls. Prayer will strengthen us, the Holy Spirit will guide us, and the witness of the church will channel our powers. As Augustine said, our souls are restless until they find rest in God. So many of us have arrived socially and professionally, but we have not yet arrived spiritually. We are like the prodigal, but still running away. We need to halt, see our sins, face up to ourselves, and turn home to God. Let us run to Him because He is our Father.

"Our responsibility" John 17:18. 11/6/55. Today, I want to talk about our responsibility to God for the church, for its present and future. *It is difficult to stir up a sense of responsibility.* There is a growing sense of fatalism among many of us, that we are not free to make choices. We give in to our animal nature and say that we aren't responsible. Some quit working and depend on the government to take care of them. In the church, the vast majority of members don't take up their responsibility for forwarding God's kingdom. They work and give as little as possible as they can get away with. *Responsibility is necessary for development.* It is appalling to see the results of rich parents giving too much to their children. Statistics show that the more we lay up for our children, the worse off they will be. We don't develop in our religious faith because we don't accept responsibility. Those who do say to the Lord, "Here I am, use me," discover that they grow in character and in ability, and the kingdom of God grows with them. There is work for all of us to do, and I believe, that after the spirit of love, the greatest need in the world today is the spirit of responsibility. *What then is our responsibility in God's work?* For one thing, we are responsible for our community. Our lives are intertwined with others in our city, nation, and world. As go the Christian congregations in Mobile, so will go the city. We are responsible for carrying Christ's message to our communities. We are stewards of God and we need to accept the responsibilities of this stewardship in our time, our work, our witness, and in our use of money. "Let the church use me."

"When God says 'No'" Acts 16:7. 12/3/55. Like a parent, God often has to say "No" to his children. He said "No" to Adam and Eve about eating the fruit, "No" to Moses on Mount Nebo, "No" to David about building the Temple, "No" to Paul about lifting the thorn in his flesh, and even "No" to Jesus who wished not to face the cross. *First, we discover that God must often say "No" in the moral realm of life.* As parents, we want to protect our children from actions that we know will only bring heartache to them and to others. The same is true with God our Father. He says "No" through moral consciousness which we call our conscience. *Second, we discover that God says "No" to false worship.* We complain when God says "No." However, we should use these occasions to examine if we are in God's will. We need to ask ourselves what is the message that God is sending me with this "No." That kind of "No" can strengthen us.

"Our Christian witness" Phil. 2:15. 2/19/56 (6/1/58). Despite all of our scientific and cultural advancements, we live in a crooked and perverse world.

What then is the Christian's place in such a world? Do we want our lives as Christians to count for something, or do we want to just look on? Our call is to be a Christian witness to the world. *What is the function of the church?* The church is a place of worship and a place of fellowship, but its chief purpose is to be a witness to a wicked and perverse world. It is Christ's mission to save, but we are to bring people into a knowledge of the saving power of Christ. *How best can we fulfill that purpose?* One way is by preaching. Another is by Christian example. Missionaries have learned that example is the best way to convince others to turn to Christ. Out of our examples grows influence. Many lay persons have the power to change society by saying "No" to evil. We must all shine as lights to the world, dispelling sin and ignorance, both in our homes and in our communities. We have so much more influence than we ever realize. God needs us as His witness.

"Concerning Christian conversion" Acts 3:19. 7/15/56. We all need conversion even though you may think that that sort of sermon is only for "bums" in the street instead of for regular church goers. Even Peter and Paul and John Wesley needed to be converted. All conversion means is a turning to God. Paul is an example of conversion. Starting out as a persecutor of Christians, Paul met Christ in a vision and in that encounter Paul was shown the error of his ways. From then on, Paul turned into the great evangelist who brought Christianity to much of the world. *Conversion does not affect all people in the same way.* For some, it is a sudden overwhelming experience, and those to whom it happens this way, remember vividly the day and the hour it occurred. This is the way it happens usually in the life of someone who has been living far from God. At other times, conversion comes through reason and study and a decision is made. A third group of people has been converted through Christian growth. They grow up in the faith. Their Christian parents showed them and taught them what it means to be a Christian from birth. This type of conversion isn't as exciting as some of the others, but it is just as real. *Elements found in Christian conversion of all types.* Conversion is God's calling and man's response to that call. Every conversion is a turning towards God. All conversions reveal the fruit of the Spirit if they are authentic.

"Concerning Christian growth" 2 Peter 3:18. 7/22/56. It is not enough to be converted, we have to also grow in our Christian life. Growth is not just about numbers; it is about personality and faith. Paul never made growth charts for the churches he founded. He, like Peter, was interested in his converts' individual growth in knowledge and grace. Conversion is just the beginning and not the end of our spiritual life. We need to press on to become the new creature, the perfect man in Christ. *How then do we grow* *in our Christian life?* The church program is geared to foster growth by its Christian education and its' preaching programs. We also grow through life's experiences. Tragedy and hardship can help us grow in a strengthened faith. Another way of growing is through cultivating some part of our Christian life through spiritual disciplines like prayer, worship, and in our practice of the virtues. Our Christianity is a practical thing that can influence all areas of our lives.

"The work of the minister" I Cor. 9:16. 9/2/56. Labor Day is a good day to consider our work as a divine calling from God. Today let us consider the work of a minister. Studies have found that many ministers face a lot of stress because their work is so scattered and varied, and that they can't focus on their main task which is to preach the Gospel. The good news the minister preaches, unlike the news in daily newspapers, never gets stale or out of date. It is news that will heal individuals and nations; news that "God is in Christ reconciling the world unto Himself." The work of the church will go on for generations, long after we are dead and forgotten, because its purpose is to preach the news of victory. The church proclaims ultimate victory over sin, over sorrow, and over evil, both in our personal and community lives. The minister is to preach this good news of the soul's safety in God. It is also the privilege of the minister to bring the good news to people concerning the abundant life for individuals and for society, promoting justice and progress in education, housing, moral and physical health, human understanding, and peace. The minister is to preach also the good news concerning eternal life; that one day we will be with our Lord. Let us all therefore preach the good news of the kingdom and dare to live the way of the good news, by being Christian in an unchristian society.

"So youth may know" 1/27/57. "These are written that ye may believe." Many youth go unprepared into the world for the moral challenges that will face them. *We all have a questing spirit.* We are all searching for something, although we can't always define just what that something is. Deep within us is a thirst for God and for the abundant life, and we start on our search when we see our need. We see our sins and short-comings as individuals and as organizations and we wish to be cleansed. We gain hope when we learn that Christ died for sinners, providing a way out of our weaknesses. This way, we learn, is through the surrender of our lives and by the acceptance of Christ's life within us. This way means "putting Christ in the saddle of our lives." The Christian faith does not take away fun and joy; it is rather the very foundation of all that is good and joyous about life. Yes, you should learn from your books and from all the wonders of the world around you, but first learn from Him who is the Creator of life and the Father of mankind.

"What Christ promises" John 14:27. 3/3/57 (5/18/57). Many people leave wills which describe how they wish that their estate be used after their death. Christ in His will to us, left us peace. "Peace I leave with you; my peace I give unto you; not as the world gives do I give to you." The gift is to "whoever will receive it." *What is the peace that Christ leaves us?* It is not freedom from war and tumult, nor is it a pampered satisfaction or selfish ease and freedom from inconveniences. It is not freedom from troubles, nor is it found in special circumstances and surroundings. Men have found His peace in riches, in poverty, in prison, and even in pain. It is simply God's peace. It is at-oneness with the Spirit of God - a God-controlled life. When a man or woman knows that God is in control of their lives and using them for a purpose, they are at peace. Others see that peace and want it. *How to get Christ's peace.* To get it, we must first empty our lives of those things that keep Christ's peace out. When we repent and turn from our sins, our guilt complexes can be replaced by peace. We claim Christ's peace for ourselves by recognizing that we are His children and that He has promised His peace to us. Finally, we have to let God take over in our lives and let Him transform us. Entering our hearts, He fills them with His peace. So with Paul we say, "Let the peace of God rule in your hearts."

"Evangelism for our day" 4/7/57. (This sermon was in preparation for the upcoming evangelistic meetings of Charles Templeton). Today, many of us shy away from emotional revivals. We are a scientific age and interested mainly if something works. True evangelism is not afraid of scientific or practical tests. Without evangelism, the church would die. Muslims conquered in the Middle East because Christian evangelism was forbidden by them. In Spain, Franco forbids the Protestants to evangelize. The purpose of evangelism is to present Christ and the love and forgiveness of God; it is not to emphasize the evangelist or preacher. The methods of Christian evangelists differ from "moral rearmament" to Quakers; from the "ashrams" of Stanley Jones to the Navigators. In this church, I would like to focus on four types of evangelism that we can do in the coming weeks. *The first is pulpit evangelism* which is represented by Charles Templeton who will be coming this next week. Much of the growth of the Church in the U.S. was because of this type of evangelism, represented by John Wesley and George Whitefield. *The second is Biblical evangelism.* It is through the Bible that we lead people to Christ. It is this Book that tells the story of Christ and of His saving grace. *The third is teaching evangelism.* Jesus commanded His disciples to go into the world and teach. One of the most effective evangelistic tools is the Sunday School which teaches children to become adult Christians. Jesus was a beloved teacher to His disciples and to the thousands who came to hear Him. *The fourth is the evangelism of personal work.* Your personal experience of and belief in the Christian gospel is the most important factor in determining your success as an evangelist in your daily contacts. Unfortunately, many of us hold off from talking about religion, even though our Christianity should be the most important thing in our lives. Personal evangelism is a person to person experience, and you can reach people that your pastor or Dr. Templeton could never reach. We as Christians have the word of life. Why do we sometimes feel so hesitant to share it with others at home, in our businesses, and in our community?

"The reward of faithfulness" I Sam. 30:24. 5/12/57. (Mother's Day). The story in the text is about the recuperation of captured family members and goods from the Amalekites by David and his men. Two hundred of David's men were left by him to guard the army's baggage, while 400 others went on to fight. In response to the complaint of some who felt that those who fought should receive the greatest share in the plunder, David replied that it should be shared equally. Each group was assigned their task, and each group fulfilled their assignment. In the church, there are people who are active in society as leaders, and others who stay at home to train and raise future citizens. Both are important and they should be rewarded equally. *It is in the home that the seed thought of religion is planted.* Faith is the most important thing that we can give a child, for our societies depend on the faith and moral character of its future citizens. This faith is first planted in the home. *Character is molded by the mother in the home.* It is at the mother's knee that the child enters his or her most important school. Character is formed through increasing freedom of choice, and by seeing a living example of high standards. These are learned from a mother. Mothers have had a huge effect on our nation through the children of character whom they have trained to be leaders. Some mothers, however, have not done their jobs so well as they are more interested in selfish pleasures or the social advancement of their children than in their spiritual advancement. They have therefore failed to plant in their children a love of God and of the church. If this is your case, then I challenge you today to do better. *How best to reward and honor our mothers.* The best way we can honor our mothers is to offer to them a true religious life on our part.

"Why work?" 2 Thess. 3:11-12. 9/1/57. Some think that they want freedom from work. Yet they are being foolish, because work brings satisfaction to life. Our desire to achieve comes only to fruition through work. There is emptiness to life without some sort of meaningful work. *What do we expect from work?* We gain a sense of security from work and also a sense of satisfaction. The best type of job is not necessarily the one that we do to live, but the one that we live to do. Thomas Edison said "I never worked a day in my life." He had so much fulfillment that it didn't seem like work to him. *How should Christians view work?* We ought to view work as a trust. When we contract to give eight hours of work, we should fulfill our contract of trust. We should also view work as a contribution. We should do our best to show in our work our Christian faith and character. Every job can be used to glorify God. All true work is sacred. Those who try to cut corners in quality, or who do things in their work that they think God would not approve, are not doing God's work. We should try to do the work best suited to our nature. In our work, we build on the past and on the achievements of others. Our work is to keep building for those who will come after us.

"What doeth thou?" John 21:21-22. 9/15/57. When we stand before God, we will stand before Him as individuals and not as a group. Jesus tells Peter in this passage not to speculate about what will happen to his fellow disciple John. Instead he should focus on his own responsibilities and assignments in the "I-Thou" relationship between him and Christ. The same message is for us today. We should worry about our own responsibilities to Christ before we meddle in the affairs of others. *Reasons that we ask the question Peter asked about John:* Perhaps it is because of friendship and anxiety for the person. That is a good reason, for we are called to love one another and to bear the burdens of others. Sometimes, however, we use our supposed concern for others to cover up our self interest. We use our question to put down others by comparing them to ourselves. We judge them unfairly. The main task that we have is to concentrate on where we are; on the life that we lead, and on the talents that we have. Peter's talents were different from John's, but God had a plan for both of their lives. In our church fellowship, God does not come to each of us in the same way or require of us the same tasks. We have in common a saving faith in Christ, but each of us has our distinctive work. Some churches stress learning with little emotion, and others are much more emotional or meditative. *Jesus gave one command to all.* Even though we are different in our experiences and talents, we are all called to follow Him. Whatever our doubts are, Jesus says to follow Him. If we do that faithfully, we will grow in both our faith and in our usefulness. We need to stop worrying about the other fellow and think about what Christ has for us to do. We need to dedicate our talents to Him and determine to follow Him. It matters not where He leads us, for we walk with the Lord.

"God was in Christ" 2 Cor. 5:19-20. 9/29/57. The nature of God is revealed in Christ. Man can discover God from many sources - from nature and from the moral code within us. We know Him by the names we give to Him like "King," "Lord," and "Father." But the perfect revelation of God is Christ. As Paul says, "God was in Christ," or as Jesus says, "If you have seen Me, you have seen the Father." This is the wonder of the Christian religion that God was in Christ, and that through His death and resurrection, He reconciled all men unto Himself. That's what makes Christianity unique. The separation that sin has caused between God and mankind has been overcome. This sin that causes bitterness and guilt in us may be indifference, immorality, selfishness, or pride. Christ has bridged the gap caused by sin and has made possible a new relationship. "While we were yet sinners, Christ died for us." This is the heart of the Christian faith. *What is our part as a church fellowship?* Paul tells us, "Entrusting to us the message of reconciliation. So we are ambassadors for Christ, God making His appeal through us." The work of the church is not to save, for only Christ can save. The church's role is to spread the good news as God's representative.

"The message of Advent" Romans 10:15. 12/1/57. Advent season is a season for evangelism, announcing the good news of Christ to the world. It began in the Old Testament when prophets like Isaiah foretold the coming of the Messiah. The announcement came to an insecure world just as ours is today. In such a time, as Paul says in Romans, "How pleasant is the coming of men with glad good news." The New Testament is a story of good news. Even though we have now heard it for 1,900 years, it is still fresh good news. It is news that God has provided a way out of our chaos; that God suffers with us; that God plans a way of triumph; that God is the Victor over life and death. Why is the news ever fresh? *The message of glad good news meets us where we are and leads us into what we can be in Christ.* The glad news is especially important for the young men and women who are home today from college. It tells us that life has a purpose, that God is alive, and that God cares. It is good news to those who are facing troubles, for it gives comfort and guidance. It is the most powerful news in all the world, for it transforms lives and gives hope. *Why then has not the world heard this announcement of the Advent of Christ who will change the world and offer abundant life?* One reason is that their minds cannot grasp it. Another reason is because the world loves darkness rather than light. There is also the fact that we haven't been effective in spreading the good news to others. May we ever proclaim that good news to our world!

"What Christianity has to offer" Eph. 3:8-9. 12/15/57. Christianity promises good will to men, but we find anything but that in today's world. Our world today is one of anxiety reflected by the stock- market, editorial writers, and news items. Some of us hope for the second coming of Christ to make things right. But Christ is already with us, as we are reminded this Christmas season by the birth of Immanuel, "God with us." What then does Christianity have to offer our world? *It offers a purpose.* Our purpose is to respond to God as a beloved child. It offers us a new life in Christ. With Christ living in us, we can fulfill God's purpose, as did Christ. *Christianity offers guidance and growth.* Once we are born again, we are not left as babes. Christianity offers us growth through Bible reading, through study, and through practice. We take Christ as our goal and model and we press on to become like Him. *Christianity offers us a new outlook.* Christians face the same hardships, sufferings, and illnesses as everyone else, but Christianity gives us the outlook of one who overcomes. It teaches us to accept what comes our way and to transform it into something that can be used to witness for Christ. *Christianity offers us renewed hope.* We live not for today, but forever. We are here to prepare for life with God forever. Let us then take all that Christianity has to offer and make it part of our lives. Then we will understand the mystery of the riches of Christ.

"Knowing ourselves" Romans 7:24. 1/26/58. Today is "Youth Sunday" and one of the marks of youth is the desire to know. Most often it is the desire to understand the world about us rather than to understand ourselves. Many of us do not know who we are and why the admonition to "know thyself" is the starting point on the road to wisdom. When we look into ourselves as Paul did, we see good and evil in conflict. "I do not understand my own actions. For I do not do what I want, but I do the very thing that I hate." *How can we best gain a knowledge of self?* We can gain it from others who often have a more accurate view of us than we do, as we so often excuse our own faults. We can examine ourselves with our reason and try to understand our motives and actions. When we do this, we find that we will grow as persons. We will also grow in our understanding of others. We will learn humility when we see ourselves as we actually are and not as we would like others to see us. This humility leads us to think of God and of our dependence on Him. We lose our delusions as to what we can accomplish by ourselves. We discover that our salvation is in God, and not in ourselves.

"When a Christian views death" I Cor. 15:55. 3/9/58. A person's soul may be viewed by the way he or she looks at death. It is the one certainty in life. *The natural man's view of death.* It brings tears and fears, for death means parting from what we love and facing the unknown which we fear. Death brings fears of punishment for the way that we have lived. Because we are so much of the world, even Christians have some of these fears and disappointments. *The Christian's view of death: There is no such thing as unknown.* Yes, we feel sorrow for the temporary parting from our loved ones, but we should not fear facing the unknown, for Christ will be there. We will be in the presence of God who knows all. We will finally see clearly what we have seen only darkly. We will not fear for the future because the future, as well as the present, is with Jesus. *There is no fear of punishment.* We know how deceitful the heart is and how far short we are of being what God wishes us to be. For that, we fear the wrath of God. The Christian looks at death, however, through the forgiving act of God. The whole message of Christianity is the message of a God who offers Himself for the sins of mankind in order that we might have life eternal and receive victory over death. As Paul says, "There is no condemnation to those who are in Christ." Christ has borne our punishment. *Finally there is fulfillment.* Death is part of the process of becoming, of completing our purpose. We believe that with death our personalities are perfected. As Paul said again, "For me to die is gain." As Christians we face the sadness of parting, but the very separation of our loved ones brings us closer to God, and heaven is therefore more real to us. Because of Christ, we fear neither death nor life, nor principalities nor powers, nor things present nor things to come. "Death is swallowed up in victory. O death where is thy victory; o death where is thy sting? Thanks be to God who gives us the victory through our Lord Jesus Christ."

"The Christian life is a campaign" Luke 4:13. 3/23/58 (3/26/58, 3/31/58, 4/17/58, 8/10/58). The Christian life is a campaign against evil. It is not just one battle, but many battles. Jesus fought many battles against the devil who tempted Him in the wilderness, and after losing there, departed to tempt Him again at an "opportune time." We, too, are in a constant campaign against evil and we must always be prepared. We can't just live in the past on some Christian experience that we had. We are called to grow in our Christian character and life. Jesus went from victory to victory over the devil and evil, and the resurrection showed that He was victor even over death itself. What is the answer that we give when we ask ourselves where we want to be in ten years in our Christian life? Is it just comfortable? Paul armed himself with the armor of God and fought the good fight throughout his life, always striving for the goal of knowing Him and becoming like Him. *What then are some of the battles ahead in the Christian life?* The battle with self is the first and foremost battle. If we could just lick the "old Adam" within us, then we could get on with fighting forces outside us. If we could win that battle, then most of the battles outside us would disappear. We also battle against world evils like materialism and "respectability" in the eyes of men. We fight against the many abuses to human rights. We battle against the world's low conception of Christ, for He is the standard by which we should measure ourselves. Both in ourselves and in our societies, we fight against evil and for the advancement of the kingdom of God. *Remember in this campaign, we fight not in our own strength, but in God's strength.* The final victory against evil is assured, because God is on our side and we do not fight alone. Let us therefore be good soldiers and face with courage the evil that is within us and without us.

"Christian character" Eph. 6:10. 4/20/58. People sometimes do terrible things and try to hide them or run away from them for awhile. But we can't run forever. *What we need is Christian character that will enable us to face up to life.* The fact of Christ's resurrection turned His disciples into persons who were now able to live victoriously and to face up to the problems of life. Christian character is the imprint of Christ's life, teachings, and resurrection on our lives. *It is this Christian character we need today to keep our work and world from going to pieces.* Today, we face immorality, crime waves, and fear on all sides, and we will disintegrate without strength of character. Our weapons of war will destroy us if men of character don't control them. Every country has fallen when the character of its people has weakened. *What does Christianity give us to build character?* Christianity gives us stamina and courage, because we know that we are not alone when we face evil. As Paul says, "I can do all things through Christ that strengthens me." Christianity gives us the fruit of the spirit – love, joy, meekness, long-suffering, kindness, etc. The love of that which is good helps to expel the love of evil in our lives. Christianity gives us a cause to serve that is greater than we are. Christ, dwelling within us, transforms us into individuals with strong characters, and as such, we make our nation strong. Sometimes the transformation happens quickly, and sometimes it happens slowly, but it does happen. There are countless examples of the truth of this in the history of Christianity. We, too, can be transformed, but we must first choose to commit our lives to Christ. Remember, we can't run away forever.

"Meeting man's needs" Philippians 4:19. 5/18/58. Statisticians estimate that today the average person has over 500 wants, of which 100 are rated as necessities. Over 32,000 items are urged on the average person by sellers, where a century ago the average was 200. Thus, meeting a person's needs might be interpreted by different people in different ways. Today, let us make our own outline of our needs for the abundant life. *It is obvious that we need food and all that food represents in the material realm.* Part of the aim of

Christian missions is to help people around the world fulfill their need for the necessary material things. *A second need that we have is for fellowship.* God has not made us to live alone to ourselves. We are social creatures and we thrive on fellowship with one another. Christianity has promoted such fellowship and sense of belonging throughout its history. It helps us to feel needed. *A third need that we have is that of faith.* We all search for something bigger than ourselves to worship and Christianity, more than other religions, supplies this need. In our faith we receive comfort and strength. *A fourth need that we have is to be cleansed from our sins and failings.* Only Christ can do that. We can't do that on our own power. *A fifth need that we have is that of a purpose.* A purpose releases our energies. It takes us out of ourselves to serve others. It gives meaning to our lives. Christ fulfills our needs and sends us into the world with a purpose, which gives meaning to our lives. Through Him we can do all things.

"Spiritual growth" II Cor. 3:18. 6/15/58. The passage describes the change that comes over the follower of Christ as he grows spiritually. "But we all with unveiled face beholding as in a mirror the glory of the Lord are changed into the same image from glory to glory as by the Lord." Today we want to talk about change and growth, and particularly of spiritual growth. In general, we see change and growth on every hand. Some change is compulsory in our physical body as we get older. We can also grow in our viewpoints as we gain more wisdom with our years. *The church offers the opportunity to grow spiritually.* The Bible talks of us growing in grace and truth. Since this type of growth is not compulsory, some Christians choose not to grow. Paul spoke of the Corinthians as still being "babes in Christ." They mainly thought of what they could get out of the church instead of what they could give. We think nothing of the selfishness of children, but in an older person such selfishness is unlovely. *Signs of growth and spiritual maturity.* Paul gave thanks for the Thessalonian Christians "because your faith is growing abundantly and the love of everyone of you for another is increasing." So growth in faith, love, grace, and knowledge are all signs of spiritual maturity. *How we gain spiritual growth.* We grow spiritually by living in the presence of Christ. His Spirit transforms us into loving and forgiving and courageous persons. Christ is reproduced in us when we commit our lives to Him and accept the responsibilities that He gives us in this life.

"Remember my bonds" Col. 4:18. 7/6/58. Not all of life is easy and there is no such thing as absolute liberty. *When Paul said "remember my bonds," he could have meant remember my limitations.* Paul wanted to spread the good news of Christ, but he was often hindered because he was in fetters or under arrest. He was also limited by illness. He had handicaps over which he had no control. He wanted others to remember these when they judged him. We also need to be sympathetic to the fetters of others so that we don't judge them too harshly. *Paul could have meant "remember that Christianity costs you something."* We should always remember the price that others have paid so that we can worship God freely today. Many have been put in prison and died so that this freedom is ours. Today, we hardly know what it means to suffer for our faith. *Paul also might be saying that since he is in bondage, think about what you can do for the faith.* When old leaders die or are imprisoned in a movement, new leaders take their place. In certain parts of the world, Christianity is in bondage today. Remembering that fact should stir us to action in our own country where we have freedom.

"And after that the judgment" Hebrews 9:27. 7/20/58. There are many different angles to the matter of judgment in the Old and New Testaments. *Old Testament judgment.* In the Old Testament, judgment is seen in relation to God's covenant with Israel, His chosen nation. Judgment against other nations was meted out when they sinned against Israel and judgment was on Israel when it broke the covenant. Also in the Old Testament, judgment was made on sin in general. God judged the world at the time of Noah, as well as Sodom for their wickedness. The prophets spoke of the "Day of the Lord," which would come in response to the wickedness of all people. In this judgment, that which was wrong would be made right, both in Israel and in the rest of the world. After the exile, the prophets began to see judgment as a time when a new age would be inaugurated in the world, a time when a new heaven and earth would be established and the Messiah would rule. *The New Testament idea of judgment.* Jesus told us not to judge others in interpersonal relationships, in the sense that we are not to be censorious of them. On the other hand, we are told to judge others by their fruits and thus avoid evil ourselves. Another concept in the New Testament is that judgment takes place every day. Our very actions judge us. What happens to us is a result of what we have done in the past; we reap what we sow. But together with these ideas of judgment, the New Testament also speaks of *a day of judgment which is the Final Judgment.* Everyone will appear before God and each of us must receive good or evil according to what we have done. Every knee will bow and every tongue will give praise to God on that day as we give accounts of our lives. Christ will be our judge, even though when He came to earth as a man, He came then not to judge, but to save. We don't know when that day will come, but come it will. *All must be judged, but there is a vast difference as we face judgment.* For those without Christ, it is a fearful thing, because they will be judged on the strength of their own lives, on what they did or failed to do in their thoughts, words, and actions. But for the Christian, it is a far different story. It is a day of victory, because our sins have been blotted out by Christ's sacrifice. So when we think of death and judgment, we ought to have a new urgency to our preaching and to the way we live our own lives. The final judgment will be the "Day of the Lord," a day of triumph for God's holiness and righteousness.

"God's concern and God's command" Is. 40:25-31. 4/5/59. There are 4,000 unclaimed dead in New York City every year who are buried in a "Potter's field." What manner of people were these in life? What led them to this sad obscure end? *Some of them probably never knew who they were.* Many of us also go through life without knowing who we are either. We don't recognize God's spark of eternity in us. Paul discovered that we were meant to be "an heir of God and a joint heir with Christ." We were created in the image of God and meant to be "sons of God." Jesus came to reveal what man in his fullness was meant to be. *Some in that Potter's field probably died before they ever learned how to live.* Like us, they might have thought that life consisted of the fulfillment of sensuous desires, of seeking power and honor, or of buying and selling. They had not found the joy of abundant living. Lots of people die before they really live and have a sense of destiny. *Some probably died knowing that they had betrayed the best in themselves.* Some of us are like Judas who betray Jesus even though He has befriended us and shown us the way to life. We betray our best selves, our talents, and our potential for good. *Some probably were persons who suffered hard blows from life, but in spite of being forgotten by the world, had carried with them a vision of God.* Good people also suffer, but they look beyond the Potter's field to God. *Do we care about the spiritual well being of these people and others like them?* People die forgotten because people do not care. Often it seems that we don't care about the spiritual needs of others. As a case in point locally: recently, we sent out 100 letters with return envelopes to canvass persons in our church willing to do visitation evangelism. Only one person out of the 100 replied. Do we really care? God cares. He knows about us and is concerned. The good news is, "God so loved the world." Let us show that we too care.

"The church within the church" Luke 22:32. 4/19/59. My thought this morning is on the fact that within the church there is a smaller group of people who act as leaven to the rest. Within most churches, there are those who are occasional members and contributors and there are those who make the Lord's work their first priority. The latter are often in prayer for the others and serve them in other ways. *There are some persons who are members of churches who are not even Christian.* There is no repudiation of the sin in their lives, faith in Christ, or newness of life. Jesus tells us that not all who say, "Lord, Lord" will enter the kingdom of heaven, but only those who do His will. There are those who use the church for selfish reasons, who are social climbers, or who go there for business purposes. These are like the "rice Christians" on the mission field who join churches for the handouts that they get. There are others who contribute nothing to the church's work or program. *But within the church are members who have caught the vision of the kingdom of God.* These are the core of the church's life. They are poor or rich, young or old, male or female, educated or uneducated, but they have one thing in common. Their faith means everything to them. *Not all of them have the same experience.* Some of these committed Christians have come to Christ by sudden conversion and others have come over many years, but they all are becoming new beings in Christ. *The church within the church has a certain work to do.* One part of their work is evangelistic, because when they have the experience of Christ's power in their lives, they want to share it. They want to help others grow in their faith and social involvement as well. We all love Government Street Presbyterian Church, but it is not enough to worship in a beautiful and historic place. It is not enough to be a nominal Christian. We have to work to become members of the church within the church in order to leaven the whole. I challenge you to do just that.

Sermons without Numbers or Dates

"The Lordship of Christ" 2 Peter 3:13. (No date). Today is Armistice Day and like our text says, we are looking for a new heaven and a new earth, for a time when world peace can become a reality. The desire for a world of peace and understanding, of order and goodness, is in every human heart. As a Christian minister, I believe that when the time comes that Jesus takes His throne as Lord of Life and Lord of economic and social activities, then we will have a new heaven and new earth. Then we will have a world of righteousness. Without the Lordship of Christ, all of our efforts to promote world peace and harmony will fail. *How can we prove that Christ's way works?* It works with the individual. Inside of us there is a civil war going on between our good side and our evil side. There is no peace in this struggle. Christ gives us peace and order when He becomes the Lord of our individual lives and of the lives of our family members. As the individual goes, so goes the world. A good society can only be produced by good individuals, so the new world has to begin with us. But it cannot begin with us unless it begins with Christ. When Christ becomes real inside us, then we are on the way to creating a new heaven and a new earth.

"Do we need the church?" (No date). The purpose of the church is to give orientation and direction. It is more than a club, more than an insurance policy for eternal life, more than a building for special events like marriage, and more than an amusement center. The church is not here to compete with civic organizations. Its purpose is to lead us to worship God in communion with others. It reveals God to us, and is a word of authority. It shows our importance to God. It reveals our sins, and teaches God's forgiveness.

"The Christian religion and the home" Deuteronomy 6:7, Pr.22:6. (No date. A Mother's Day sermon). A house is very different from a home. There are certain qualities that make a home. We stress today the physical side of raising children, of protecting them from germs, and of giving them good food to make their bodies strong. We stress security, both physical and financial for our children, and take out insurance policies for their education and marriage expenses. We supply our children with the material things of life, but sometimes without giving them the spiritual resources that they will need. Too many material goods can destroy a child's initiative and character and some children don't know the meaning of self-denial. *Something else is needed besides the material.* The Christian religion furnishes us the character that enables us to use rightly our material blessings. Some traits of this character are self discipline, vicarious suffering for others, and contemplation of the goal, the purpose, and the ultimate meaning of life. Parents who instill these traits in their children will be honored.

"The lifting power of our religion" Psalm 145:4. (No date). Man has discovered the atomic power to destroy, but has often ignored the spiritual power of God to lift us up. Those who survived best the horrors of the concentration camps were priests and other spiritual people whose hope was in God. Let us look at some of the ways Christianity has lifted people up through the centuries. *It has lifted nations of people.* It is easy for us to forget our debt to the Christian faith which has done away with, or reduced practices, of witch craft, of child abandonment and sacrifice, of the denial of basic human rights, or of the desire for revenge against defeated enemies. *It has lifted the individual.* Religion is a great power that comes to help us in our anxieties and troubles. David calls God "a shield." Our religion lifts us up in our sickness, sorrow, loneliness, disgrace, and other trouble. It lifts us up when the power of sin is too much for us to combat alone. *How the uplifting power of God comes to us.* It seems to come to us from within. The kingdom of God is within us; that is where we sense God's presence.

"Obedience to discipline brings freedom" Matt. 7:13-14. (No date). The gate that leads to life is narrow and those who find it are few. One of the principles of life is that obedience to discipline must precede genuine liberty and life. Sometimes we forget this rule and cast aside customs and rules. Our shortcuts, however, often lead to misery. We all know that to be a success in any area of life, we must be disciplined. The great musician was first a student doing his or her scales. The great painter practices hours and hours every day drawing. The Bible scholar spends years studying the text. The star football player becomes a star because of the constant repetition of details and body building. *Obedience to discipline creates power.* The sun can be concentrated to burn holes in metal, and by the concentration of our mental power, we can also achieve great results. Dwight L. Moody, who concentrated his life on doing the will of God, was able to bring many to conversion. It is only through the narrow way of discipline that we have freedom. Paul writes "where the Spirit of the Lord is, there is Liberty." The Holy Bible that we give our children today as they go to another level in Sunday school is a living guide to the road of life. We should follow Christ's teaching and shun the broad way and choose the narrow one that leads to life.

GENERAL TALKS

"Why every fireman should be an active Christian" (Talk to volunteer firemen). Amos 4:11. 3/1/36. God plucks us from the fire of evil and of death. He also saves us from inner fires of lust and the fires generated by an uncontrolled tongue. Fires run rapidly through our lives and destroy them. Like kids we set fires to have fun, but they can get out of our control. We need the church to save us from fires and to make us better firemen. Firemen both put out fires and prevent them from starting. Firemen need the church and the church needs firemen. The fireman and the Christian serve others everywhere. They learn discipline and obey the orders of others. We need committed active firemen and committed active Christians. We are all, and not just ministers, called to be spiritual firemen, as flames are everywhere.

"The art of being a gentleman" (Talk to various fraternities). 11/11/37 (2/7/38, 2/28/38, 9/10/40). There are many definitions of a gentleman. Some are based on manners and others on social life. Fraternities help shape social life, dress, etc. Fraternities can also harm boys with too much emphasis on drinking. A gentleman is one who plays the game of life fairly. He is one who puts back into life more than he takes out. The church plays an important role in making a person into a gentleman.

"What are you gaining from college?" (Talk to Y.M.C.A. cabinet). 4/8/37. College is for preparing for your life's work. You and your parents have made sacrifices for you to be here. Rummaging through the attic at home, I found an album of my sister from college days full of memories of dances and beaus. Now it is dusty and forgotten. Make sure that what you collect from college is not like this forgotten album. Collect knowledge and experience that is important and that you can use daily. *For example, education.* I am not talking just about learning facts and getting degrees, but gaining meaningful insights about life. *For example, friendship.* Don't just try to be popular, but seek friends who will lift you up and inspire you. Education and friendship as well as organizations like the YMCA and YWCA help us form a living philosophy of life.

"Sacrifices for a college education. Is it worth it?" 2/1/38. (Chapel talk at Mississippi State). Your parents have sacrificed so that you can get a college education, but many of you may not take advantage of the time you are in school to pursue knowledge. It is certainly worth getting an education for the value added to your life and work. (He gives many examples of people who sacrificed for an education and then went on to do important work in science, business, arts and the ministry).

"Installation service for Starkville Woman's auxiliary officers" 3/12/39 (5/14/54). As you come to serve the church, let us take inspiration in the cross of Christ and bring to Him the following qualities: *Bring the spirit of surrender.* Surrender to Jesus is the pre-requisite for effective service. *Bring the spirit of loyalty.* How noble it is to remain true to Christian principles when they are sometimes ridiculed. *Bring the spirit of communion.* Through communion with God we gain strength from Him. *Bring the spirit of patience.* So often Christ had to exercise patience with His disciples and you too will need much patience in your work. *Bring the spirit of faith.* Let us believe in our organization, its goals, and the work that it does for Christ. Now let each of you light the candles signifying your commitment to surrender, loyalty, communion, patience, and faith.

"Stewardship of Life" (Young people's conference). 3/31/39. If a few young people totally dedicated their lives to Christ, they could change the whole South. To be a steward of God means to know Him, to give yourself to Him, and to work for Him. Many people say that they believe in God, but He is a living reality to very few. An experiential knowledge of God will make us into His stewards. If we want to feel God's presence, then we need to act in service to Him and to others, for we are told that everyone who loves is born of God and knows God.

"The technique of worship" (YMCA). 4/5/39. We usually get the most out of what we understand best. A football player gets a lot more out of football than someone who doesn't know the game. Let us therefore try to understand worship. First there is preparation for worship, either before the service or when we walk in. It is a period of silence. The responses begin the service and then there is the singing of a hymn. I recommend that you try to apply the words of the hymn to your life. There is also the anthem by the choir. Music helps lift our thoughts to God. The sermon is a very important part of the service and I suggest that you listen more in a worshipful mood rather than a critical one. Try to find something in the sermon that you can apply to yourself. The final step is application. We must use what we have received if we really want to learn and grow. As someone said, "impression without expression means depression."

"Talk for Boy Scouts" 6/1/39. I will talk first to the Scouts and then to you parents. What does "Scout" mean to you boys? To me the S stands for spiritual, superior, stupendous. C stands for curiosity, courtesy, climbing to higher levels. The O means to me obedience to God, to country, and to the wisdom of your parents. U stands for useful. The T, above all, means trustworthy. Now to the parents, what does the word "Scout" mean? S stands for the support and enthusiasm of the parents. The C stands for community. The O stands for organization in the sense of pulling together as one. U is for the unity of Protestants and Catholics and Jews who work hand in hand in scouts and also for the unity of races. Finally there is the letter T which stands for the training that you parents should give your children in the home.

"Devotional for 'Future Farmers of America'" I Cor. 3:1-11. 7/18/39. Russian authorities were trying to teach young people that there was no God and so chose two fields side by side to compare to each other. One was designated "Man's field" and was plowed, planted, and weeded. The other was" God's field" and was left alone. As one would expect, "Man's field" produced a beautiful crop while "God's field" only produced weeds. The teacher said that this showed that there was no God. However, the teacher failed to explain where the soil and seed and water came from, how the seed sprouted, and who created and gave the strength to the students who took care of the field. Truly God must be taken into consideration, as it is God who provides 95% of the materials and energy for a crop. We are partners with God. He does His best work with us, and we are helpless without Him. When I was 10 or 11, I worked for a $1.00 a week for a Gulf Gasoline distributor in Meridian, Miss. The money meant little, but what was important was that this distributor had some stationary printed and listed me, J.C. Frist, as his Junior Partner. That made me happy and proud. We should be even more proud when we think that we are partners with God.

"Trophies" (Chapel talk at Mississippi State) 9/19/39 (11/1/39). The trophy room and "Hall of Fame" room at the college are filled with tangible memories of glory days at the school in many sports. When you leave here, you will take your own trophies, some tangible and some not. One trophy is a real education. I don't mean just a diploma, but a mind open to knowledge. Education helps one find his true self. Another trophy is friendship. Treasure these two trophies for life.

"Talk for O.A.K. fraternity" (Mississippi State College). 12/4/39. There are three classes of O.A.K. members. There are the active members who are in school; the associate members who have graduated; and the honorary members. There are no inactive members of O.A.K. because the active members are involved in leadership positions in the school; the associate members and honorary members are active in leadership positions in their community, and thus bring honor to the fraternity. Our task as O.A.K. members is to turn ourselves into the high type of individual this badge represents, working as leaders in many diverse groups. O.A.K. is a unique organization because it desires to instill in its members a love for character and a desire to help the whole institution. O.A.K. men are well rounded men in studies, athletics, friendship, and extra-curricular activities like religion and fraternities. Welcome to the fraternity.

"Devotional talk for all extension workers of State" (Outline of talk at Mississippi State College) John 6:68. 12/16/39. In a house of mirrors, we often butt into an image of ourselves in our search for a way out. The same is true in life. Christ is the way we should follow; false ways reflect our selves.

 "Look to this day" (Starkville High School). John 11:9. 3/12/40 (6/16/45, 5/25/54, 5/30/59). Look to today, for yesterday is a dream and tomorrow is a vision. Use your present time to the fullest. Do the job at hand and that will make tomorrow's tasks easier. Jesus met each day with its duties. He asked, "Are there not 12 hours in the day?" (A long story from Tolstoi's "Twenty three Tales" is told to illustrate that there is only one time that is important – now).

"The ethical principles of Jesus on a college campus" (Notes for talk at Montreat College). 7/1/40. Ethical problems are of three sorts: One type, those that arise in the choice between right and wrong. Whether to cheat or not is this type of choice. A second type are those that arise in the choice between two wrongs, such as in choosing the lesser evil over the greater evil. Then there is the third type, the choice between two rights, the best over the good. Because of time restraints, I want to concentrate today on Jesus' ethical principles to love God and to love our neighbor as ourselves and on His admonition that our righteousness should exceed that of the Pharisees. We will look at them narrowly in our actions towards fellow students and in our attitudes to the moral laws that govern the campus. One ethical problem that we have in the South that we are not meeting head on is that of race. Most of us as pastors or students are not heroes in applying the ethical principles of Jesus to race relations. (Some other examples involving fraternities and other situations are also discussed).

"Christianity on the campus" (Y.M.C.A. retreat). 9/7/40. Today, more than ever, we need a virile Christianity on the campus. We need it for the stability it gives to us in an insecure world. We need it for the hope it gives us, and because it helps keep us morally straight and spiritually awake. We need it because it challenges us to be the best we can, and to be responsible persons aiding others. We need Christianity on campus that is real and not just pretend. *What can we do as Christians on campus?* Some of the situations where we as Christians can witness are in our moral life and in repudiating gambling, excess drinking, and indifference. We also can witness in how we deal with class and race differences both on and off the campus. This is your campus and you can help make it Christian or you can choose to do nothing.

"Preparing for the arrival of the Minister" (Talk he was asked to give to the church at Tupelo, Mississippi). 9/20/40. Encourage the new minister by writing him notes. Leave flowers in the manse for him and his family for when they arrive. Introduce members and be patient at first with his forgetting names. Don't criticize either his sermons or his family or tell others that you don't like him. Help him with his library. Don't spoil him and don't pay him extras beyond his salary. Remember that your minister is a human being and needs the comradeship of other men. He makes mistakes, so don't expect the impossible. Remember that he has many diverse duties, from preaching to administration, to being a pastor, and in some duties he will be better than he is in others. Hold up his position and message with respect. Expect much from him in the preaching of the word in all its purity. Expect him to stick to his called work and not to be an expert in other things like politics. Don't limit him by what he can say in the pulpit and don't limit his work in the greater church and community. Limit what you require of him in attending social functions so that he has time for the ministry.

"Money" (Outline of talk to Y.M.C.A. cabinet) 10/9/40. Some might ask, why talk to college students about money as they have none? Why not talk about it, I say. We spend it every day, either ours or someone else's. Our use of money is a revelation of our character. Money can harm us if we don't have the right attitude to it. Don't let it lower your ideals or let it play too prominent a role in your life. Money can of course also help us. We need to conquer money before it conquers us.

"Thanksgiving talk" Mississippi State Chapel 11/21/40, Tampa University 11/22/44. There are many reasons for ingratitude, but I would like to talk about two of the main ones. *Thoughtlessness.* Thousands of letters were written to Santa Claus last year through the post office asking for presents, but they only had one thank you letter. We take our prosperity and freedoms too much for granted. *Selfishness.* We sometimes want what we want for ourselves, even if it means that the other person doesn't get anything. Gratitude, however, creates good will. Just think of how your parents or teachers would be uplifted if you sent them a letter thanking them. On a national level, we should be thankful for so many things, like our freedom, our security, our heritage, and our education. The best way of showing our thankfulness is to work towards keeping America free and great.

"Growth in education" I Tim.4:11-16. (County superintendent's meeting). 4/41. (Mobile leadership school) 10/10/49. New discoveries are constantly being made in science and in other fields, including education. Religion and education should work together to create new people. In both, if we do not use the knowledge that we have, we run the risk of losing it. We should never feel that we have arrived and stop growing. Education means growth in both attaining and using facts. For all of the erudition present here, we all need to sit at the feet of God and grow in grace and knowledge.

"The present and the future of man" (Starkville woman's club). 5/43. One third of Americans do not know why we are in a war at the moment. Some say it is because of Hitler and Mussolini, but what we are fighting goes deeper than just them. *One of the deeper causes of the present war and all wars is selfishness.* This means that we look after our own national interests above all else. While America is not as imperialistic as some other nations, it, too, looks at its self interest. We are selfish when we insist on isolationism or when we refuse to forgive. If we don't forgive, the seeds of a future war will be planted. *What faces us in the future?* Our leaders are planning for the future so that we will not have new revolutions starting when the war is over. This planning involves seeing that people have food, employment, and peace. As they plan, they will have to deal with people with both their strengths and weaknesses. They will have to try to promote the good and arrest the bad in our nature. We have to change if we want a better world. Organizations such as your club, along with churches and synagogues, can help us change people for the better.

"The fact of God's guidance" 11/1/43 (12/28/49). Radio address. We plan our lives in detail professionally and socially, but how well do we plan them religiously? Today I challenge you to take a religious theme and think about it and apply it all day. Let us choose today the religious fact of God's guidance. The Bible is full of promises about God's guidance. The Lord is our Shepherd, and as Jesus promised, the Spirit of Truth will guide us into all Truth. We find the guidance of the Spirit when we surrender our day and our will to God to be led by Him and to no longer insist on our own will. We find His guidance when we turn away from evil towards the Light. Of course God has given us common sense to make decisions, but in other ways, He will open up our day for us offering opportunities of service and showing us His presence in our lives. God will see us through the day if we let Him.

"The abundant life" 11/2/43. (1/23/48). Radio address. By the abundant life, we mean more than cars, jobs, and luxury goods. We believe that such a life can only come through Jesus Christ. Jesus says "I am come that they might have life and that they might have it more abundantly." The abundant life is for all of us as God is no respecter of persons. In fact, it is more apt to be found in a peasant's cottage than in a king's palace. This day we will all have ample opportunity to taste of the abundant life, to be kind and friendly, to encourage, and to serve others. How comforting it will be at the end of the day if you use your opportunities to make life more pleasant for others. We all have an equal share of minutes and hours today to use well. We have the power that God has given us as individuals to make a difference in the lives of others. More importantly, we have His power behind us to supply our every need. When we realize this and draw on His power, we will find life in its abundance. We must practice the abundant life, seeing the spark of divinity and goodness in others. Jesus was able to see the good in people like Mary Magdalene when others only saw evil. Jesus can help us take the scales off our eyes to see the beauty of God's world and lead us into a more abundant life. "O Christ, speak Thy encouraging word to us today that we may follow Thee into the way of abundant living."

"Practicing Christian friendship, human and divine" 11/3/43. (1/21/48, 7/14/54). Radio address. The Bible contains a record of beautiful friendships between individuals and between God and individuals. Jesus says "Ye are my friends if ye do whatsoever I command. These things I command you that ye love one another." How well do we do in fulfilling this command? Do we have a friendly smile and offer hospitality to the many people who are lonely in our city? Do we offer understanding to those who are cross, and service to those who are in need? When we give friendship we usually receive it back. We cannot get along without our friends. But most of all, we need the friendship that God offers us. He laid down His life for us in Jesus and there is no greater love than this. The friendship of God is the deepest fact of all life and it gives us security of spirit.

"Practicing serenity of soul" 11/4/43 (7/15/54). Radio address. In our busy lives, how do we find peace? In work, government, business, and even in family life, it is hard to find peace. Neither can most of us force our will and minds to be rid of anxiety. Man's desperation, however, is God's opportunity. Jesus in His will to his disciples didn't leave them money or thrones, but He left them peace. "Peace I leave with you, my peace I give unto you." We need to prepare ourselves for its inflowing power by finding some moments during the day for a quiet time with God in prayer and meditation. In those times, remember the good and give thanks for it. We need to empty ourselves of our sins and to put our trust in a greater Power. To do the will of Jesus is perfect rest.

"Practicing the love of God" 11/6/43 (7/16/54). Radio address. We have been trying to practice the Christian life daily this week. Practicing the love of God is the kernel of how we should live. Christian love to others is inspired by the love of God for us. The love which fulfills our life is not the love that we receive, but the love that we give to others. Like a mother with her child, our focus should be on giving love without thought of repayment. In life, those we admire the most are those who give themselves for others. In loving others, we find joy and peace. "God is love, and he that loveth is born of God." Let God control your thoughts and life and then love others with His love. Through this love, we find abundant life.

"The orders of the day to our young people" 3/22/45. (Given at a social event for church young people). I didn't want to tell corny jokes or preach to you a sermon so I let my sub-conscious decide last night how I was going to address you today. During the night I dreamed I was in a prisoner of war camp run by both the Japanese and Germans. All the prisoners were starving, dead bodies were left to decompose, and all we could think about was escape. There was no laughter or fun – just defeat, despondency, and death. I was so glad to awake. But then I had to wonder what did this dream mean? How could it possibly be the message I was to bring to you young people who have gathered for a good time banquet? Maybe the dream meant that we should value those who have suffered so that we could have freedom of worship and an easy life of laughter and opportunities in America. But spiritually, what the dream meant to me was that we are engaged in a war against evil and that sin has made many of us into prisoners of war. Nothing could be worse than to let evil win and throw us into its filthy camps of captivity. That captivity would be our lot, were it not for the freedom Christ offers us. Christ calls us into active service as soldiers in His army. *What should be our reaction?* Freed prisoners of war break down in tears of gratitude and the American flag takes on new meaning to them. Many such freed prisoners will turn to fighting against the insanity of war. Others will return to their lives with new enthusiasm. *But what about our spiritual reaction?* As Christians, we take so much for granted. If it were not for Christ, we would still be under the power of evil. It was Christ who gave us freedom of government, of the individual, and who advanced the status of women. Name any good, and it was Christ's influence and principles that made it better. Since we have always had these goods, we sometimes forget about them and don't value them so much. So today, I challenge you to reflect on who you are and all that you have. Look at the past of sin from which you have been freed. Look at the present with all of your privileges and opportunities. I challenge you each to a new determination to show your gratitude to God for all that you have by giving your best to your Master. The charge to you is "Onward for Christ." Let us be as brave in our fight against spiritual evil as with the physical enemies that face our nation.

"The church and the peace to come" Given to the Tampa Torch Club 3/26/45, and Tampa branch of the A.A.U.W. 11/10/45. (This is a long and detailed paper describing many peace conferences and points. The following is the barest summary.) We have been at war, but the primary work of the Church is peace and goodwill. *It is only natural that the church should lead in plans for peace.* World brotherhood is important to the whole life and program of the Catholic and Protestant Church and to Judaism. We must sway our fellow citizens so that the Congress will vote in favor of the establishment of a world body promoting world peace. The church's concerns for justice for all nations has been heard by the government, particularly through John Foster Dulles. *First, what are the proposals put forth by the English church? (which has suffered far more than the U.S. church.)* Before the end of the war, the leaders of the Anglican and Catholic churches made 10 proposals for establishing a lasting basis for peace. These proposals were that extreme inequality in wealth should be abolished; every child should have an education; the family should be safe-guarded; earth's resources should be seen as a gift of God to all and should be conserved for future generations; the right to life and independence of all nations should be safe-guarded; the sense of divine vocation should be restored to daily work; disarmament should be promoted; the real needs and just demands of peoples and nations be considered; international institutions should be established to see that agreements are carried out; and peace settlements should be established in the light of divine laws. *Now, what are the specific proposals presented by the church in the U.S.?* There have been a number of meetings of churchmen to discuss this topic. Some of the most important proposals put forward by American churches are the concern for the welfare of all peoples; the protection of minorities and disarmed populations; no punitive reparation; no humiliating decrees of war guilt; no arbitrary dismemberment of nations; the delegation of powers to international institutions for the resolution of disputes between nations. The quest for private gain should not disregard human welfare and nations should cooperate with each other. Other items stressed the need for understanding between races, the freedom of religion, and the protection of minorities. In 1943, a committee of Protestant, Catholic, and Jewish leaders came up with a seven point declaration saying that a just peace must be based on our subjection to God and His moral law; that humans who are in the image of God must be respected; that the progress of colonial peoples to independence should be promoted; that minorities should be respected, that international law and institutions should be established; that economic collaboration be promoted; and that we should put our own households in order morally and economically. Later, a conference of 450 interdenominational church leaders met under the leadership of Dulles to discuss the Dunbarton Oaks proposals. In condensed form, it said that the world organization should develop and operate under international law; no nation should be allowed to sit in judgment on its own case; the character of the world organization should be susceptible to amendment; a agency should be set up to promote the autonomy of dependent areas; a commission on human rights and freedoms should be established; all nations willing to accept the obligations of membership should be invited; and the long range purposes of the Atlantic charter should be reaffirmed. Along with these proposals and gatherings many individual churches have met on the subject of peace. The church has had an important role in educating the public about the need for and the issues involved in the establishment of a structure promoting permanent peace. *Obstacles that stand in the way of a just and durable peace.* First, many people who have suffered much have revenge in their hearts. Two, there is the desire for reparations. Third, there is the problem of boundaries. Fourth, there is the problem of Russia. Fifth, there is the problem of colonial possessions. Sixth, the relationship between the East and the West is a problem and is an economic question as well as a racial one. Seventh, what should be done with the Axis, our enemies. The church has a huge role in promoting peace by stressing the sovereignty of God, the principles given by Jesus to the world, the rule of moral laws, and the rights of individuals.

"Writing materials of the early church" 4/24/46. (This study is in outline form and deals with the making of the Bible). The letters of the New Testament traveled greatly between the churches before being gathered. The first collection of Paul's letters was made 25 years after his death. Paul's letter to the Romans played a huge role in transforming the world and the lives of Christian leaders like Augustine, Luther, Wesley, and Barth. (He then examines the history of papyrus and how it was made and used as well as the history of the reed as a writing instrument. Scrolls were inconvenient to read so the papyrus codex was developed. Also leather parchment vellum was used).

"Future outlook of today" James 4:13-14. 1/19/47. (Hillsboro High school baccalaureate) How difficult it is to see correctly into the future. Looking into my own high school annual with its pictures and predictions for students, I see how much styles have changed and the predictions made about classmates were usually very wrong. One bright young ladies' man, with a great future before him in high school, ended up in a mental hospital; another with infidelities that wrecked a promising political career. As students, we did not see the war coming or the depression. We can't see into the future, but we can plant certain seeds in our character today that will bear fruit tomorrow. *Look to the future, but look aright.* Take God into account as you look into the future. Don't put off for tomorrow the work that needs to be done today. Make provisions for the future in savings and in planning. Don't be like the farmer who depletes his soil for a present gain without thinking of future harvests. The fundamental teaching of the Bible in regard to the future is that the seed that is planted today will bear fruit tomorrow. A good seed will bring forth good fruit and an evil seed, bad fruit. By urging you to live a clean moral life of responsible choices in the present, I'm not trying to limit your happiness, but to increase it in the future. *What is the look ahead for these young people?* An age of wonder with scientific advances is in front of you. But these advances must be controlled by the right attitudes of mind and heart. The seeds of the Christian spirit must be planted today in order to guide you tomorrow. In this sense, the future is now.

"Sincerity of purpose" Luke 9:51. (Agnes Scott Baccalaureate). 5/30/48 (6/4/48, 5/27/51). (Similar to the "Whither" sermon). Normally, Baccalaureate preachers feel that they have to preach long and lofty, erudite sermons to their audiences, given the weight of the occasion. I heard a lot of them as chaplain at Mississippi State. Because of that, I decided that if I were invited to preach such a sermon, I would preach a simple message, as if to young people in my church. I would not try to impress the faculty. This is the only sort of sermon that I know how to preach. Up until now, you have been largely under the protection of your parents. But now you will be standing on your own and facing an exciting future. You must determine the direction your life will take. *Life must have sincerity of purpose.* Those people who have most lifted mankind are people driven by a definite purpose. *But it must be a purpose guided by knowledge.* We need to join knowledge and competence in a particular profession with human wholeness and civic consciousness because that helps us work together in cooperation with others. *What purpose then do you intelligently choose?* You can do no better than Jesus did by linking His life with God's eternal purpose in the service of His fellow men.

"Your life, a gift for service" Gal. 6:10. (Jackson High graduation). 5/6/51 (10/14/56, 11/12/56, 5/10/59, 5/24/59). In our cynical age, we wonder what life is all about. Well, it is about service to God and to others. (He gives many examples). Let us remember in our self-sufficient age that we need the strength of Christ in us in order to serve others. You cannot be a good nurse or Christian businessman or woman without being grateful to God for your life as a gift of God. You will need to turn to Him for the guidance, comfort, and strength that you need to serve others. (He tells the story of Alexander Fleming, who as the gardener's son saves the life of his master's son, young Winston Churchill who was drowning. Later, he was helped to get his medical degree by the grateful, wealthy family, and in his professional life, he discovered penicillin. Fleming later saved Churchill again in Egypt from pneumonia with his discovery). Life is full of less dramatic opportunities for service to others, and those who do so will find joy in living.

"Today's decision is tomorrow's destiny" Luke 9:51. (Baccalaureate sermon at Southwestern in Memphis 5/31/53, Gulf Park College 2/25/58 and at McCallie School in Chattanooga when Johnny graduated 5/31/59, each time revised). One of the problems of today is that we do not know "whither" we are going with our lives. We have no goals. By answering this question "whither?" for yourself, you will help determine your future destiny. I am not talking just about what job you will have, but about what noble purpose will guide your life. *Too many of us belong to the 'if' society.* "If I had only done this or that," we say. But we cannot change the past. If we have a noble purpose, some of these minor decisions we make will not matter so much. Christ's purpose was to be God's sacrificial lamb, and He headed to Jerusalem to fulfill that purpose. It was the purpose that mattered, not that He was a carpenter or a fisherman. *Destiny hinges on the purpose you have.* You want to choose a higher purpose that will not be compromised, no matter what life throws at you. *What then ought to be our purpose?* It should have two elements: One is the desire to serve our fellow man in whatever we do. The second is to recognize God as our partner in this undertaking. Life will be a struggle, but it can also be exciting as we work with God to bring in His kingdom.

"The story of Easter" (Given to Tommy's Westlawn 3rd grade class). 5/15/54. When you were small children, Easter was a happy time of finding Easter eggs and chocolate and dressing up in new clothes. It also meant going to full churches. But the real meaning of Easter is not this. It is the new life that is offered us by the resurrection of Jesus. It's God's way of telling us not to fear death because He is on the other side. I have in my pocket some tiny mustard seeds. It's hard to believe that you can plant these in the soil and they grow into a plant. God assures us that we are like these little seeds, because when we die, we go to a more beautiful life and become the people God wants us to be. In our families, we know about death, maybe of a grandfather or grandmother. Easter tells us that they have gone to a beautiful home. Easter is a time of joy, because it shows that Good will conquer evil. Let us thank God for Easter.

"The promise of our priesthood" (Given to the General Assembly of the Presbyterian Church U.S.). Jer. 31:34. 6/30/54. Some people don't like to pray to God because they "don't know Him." Instead, they want others like priests to pray for them as an intermediary. In the Old Testament, God chose Israel as a kingdom of priests to other nations. In the New Testament, Jesus opened the door so that all men and women could be priests with direct access to God. The priest reaches out to God for others and reveals God to others. That should be our role today. People should be able to see God in our lives. Today, we as priests don't make sacrifices of animals because in the new covenant God expects not the sacrifice of animals, but the sacrifice of ourselves. This is the sacrifice our High Priest Jesus Christ gave so that we might be cleansed of all our sin and become like Him. May we all practice the presence of the Living Christ in our lives.

"What are you worth?" (A talk for the men of the Northern Mississippi Presbytery). (No date). We ask the worth of everything but of ourselves. What we see in man determines his worth. If you just look at the physical make-up of the human body, its' worth would be about $.98. *What are you worth to yourself?* Our worth is also not in how much property or money that we have. Jesus says, "What does it profit a man if he gains the whole world and loses his own soul?" Are we producing false values for ourselves or eternal values like goodness, beauty, and making the world happier for others? The greatest worth you can create in yourself, that will bring you real satisfaction and joy, is a clean heart, a pure mind, and a conscience free of evil worries. *What are you worth to your family?* I imagine that we men are pretty worthless to our wives in some practical things like doing the dishes, taking care of the children, and mowing the yard. But you can have infinite worth in the instilling of character in your children and in inspiring them. Does your child look to you for guidance and faith, or does he or she look through you and see hypocrisy. *What are you worth to your church?* Do you feel that all you need to do is to put a nickel in the offering as rent on your heavenly mansion, or do you take an active part in the activities of the church? Do you always complain, or do you seek to help others in their spiritual growth? Laymen, when they are dedicated to Christ, have had a tremendous effect on the work of the church in spreading the Gospel. *What are you worth to God?* We know the value God has placed on us because He sent His Son to die for us. God considers every man and woman of infinite worth. But what do we produce for God in return? If we put God first, our productive value would soar. Think of how God made us just below the angels. When we put God first, we become more useful to Him, to our church, to our family, and to ourselves.

"How to make life worth living today" (No date). In the midst of this war, so many hopes have been dashed, and because of that, we would expect people to suffer from depression. Yet in Britain, which has endured heavy bombing, the spirit is good. Why do some become depressed while others are lifted out of themselves to a spirit of happiness in bad times? There are three types of maturity: physical, intellectual, and emotional. In terms of happiness, emotional maturity has the most effect. *It seems to me that five roads lead to emotional maturity; that make life worth living.* The *first* way is to accept our own imperfections. All of us are handicapped in one way or another. We are partly good and partly bad, and we are called to grow even though we know we can never be perfect. The *second* road is to develop a mature conscience. A childish conscience accuses us for things that are not forbidden to us as adults. Life becomes a burden when we see accusing fingers pointing at us on all sides. The tragedy is that the protecting "thou shall not" of childhood becomes a prison wall for us when we are mature. Only when we are free of this prison, and develop our own healthy and mature conscience, can life be made worth the struggle. A *third* way to make life worth living is to develop courage and a combative spirit. We need to harness our energy to make things happen, to fight injustice, disease, and evil in all of its forms. The *fourth* way to make life worth living is to adopt a long range scale of values. We have to learn to give up momentary satisfactions for more lasting pleasures. We have to learn to measure a present pain against a future pleasure and a present pleasure against a future pain. This is true not only for us as individuals, but for humanity in general. One generation benefits from the sacrifices of a previous generation, or suffers from their excesses. The *fifth* way to make life worth living is the way of love - to have a relationship of friendliness with others and the capacity to consider their interests as well as our own. Some see others only as an audience to give admiration, praise, and affection. The effect of this view of others is unhappiness. Egocentricity is a tragic cause of pessimism and cynicism and can become a symptom of mental illness. It gives a false idea of the world and of others. The paradox of the world is that he who wishes to find himself must lose himself. He must submerge himself in ideals and causes outside of and greater than himself. The secret of success in the world is to place oneself in service to loved ones and great causes, and most of all to God. Like Isaiah, even though we are men of unclean lips, we say to God, "Here am I, send me." Suffering we may undergo, failure we shall encounter, tragedy often will be our lot. Yet we can create an unconquerable human spirit that proclaims in spite of it all and through it all that, "Life can be made worth living."

"Here I am, send me" (A multi-day devotional for a conference of young people). (No date). <u>Day One</u>. *Who calls us?* Isaiah 40:21-31, I Cor.3:9-21. The sovereign God who created all things has called us to be co-laborers with Him. Think about it! <u>Day Two</u>. *Why answer the call?* Isaiah 1:1-18, I Tim. 4:11-16. Our faith usually comes first through our parents and church, but as young people we put it to the test. As someone said, "Faith is not trying to believe something regardless of the evidence. Faith is daring to do something regardless of the consequences." <u>Day Three</u>. *Am I worthy?* Isaiah 6:1-7, Luke 18:9-14. Facing a Holy God, our natural self answers "no." But our Christian self answers "yes." Christ died for us even though we were sinners. He knows our weakness and our sins. Our worth grows when we confess our sins, seek to profit from them, and then turn ourselves over to Jesus. God knows, God cares, and God forgives. <u>Day Four</u>. *Have I counted the cost?* Isaiah 40:1-11, Luke 15: 28-33. Jesus calls us to forsake all for Him and people like Dwight L. Moody, John Wesley, and Stanley Jones, to name only a few, have done just that and become incredibly useful to others. <u>Day Five</u>. *How shall I serve?* Isaiah 53:1-12, Phil. 2:5-13. The Christian serves in the Spirit of Christ, forgetting selfish desires. It is in the world that we must serve Him -- the world of our home, our school, and our social relationships. Later we will serve Him in our business and professional life. Let us pray that we will serve Him with His Spirit in all the departments of our lives. <u>Day Six</u>. *What help shall I have?* Isaiah 43:1-13, Eph. 6:10-17. We soon find that we need help from God to follow through in our Christian life. We cannot do it alone. We are armed with the help of Christ's Spirit. As we love God and serve Him, we find that we can do all things through Christ His Son who strengthens us. <u>Day Seven</u>. *What are the obstacles before us?* Isaiah 59:1-8, Rev. 3:14-22. The greatest obstacle to answering God's call is one's own self. Selfishness lulls us into an attitude of not caring. Another obstacle is our unwillingness to go all out for Christ – to confess our sins and to go the extra mile in service. <u>Day Eight</u>. *What is my responsibility?* Isaiah 5:1-7, Luke 13:6-10. We have all had a week of rich experience and fellowship. Think how much you have been privileged and think also what you plan to undertake for Christ when you return home. Can you sincerely pray this prayer? "Lord Jesus, today I want to re-dedicate myself anew to Thee. I thank Thee for these men and women who have led me into a clearer understanding of the Christian life. In all humility, recognizing my faults and failures, I desire to serve Thee. At this moment, I mean it with all my heart when I pray, 'Here am I, use me.' In Jesus' name, Amen."

NOTES FOR PRAYER MEETING TALKS

Many of these are in outline form and handwritten.

"The efficient church" 9/1/43. (PM1).

"A Christmas talk on when Christ was born" 11/23/37. (PM 2).

"Christ as prophet, priest, and king" Heb. 7:19-28. 12/28/37. *Christ is a prophet* in that He reveals to us the word and will of God for our salvation. He reveals God to man, man to himself, and God's kingdom to man. He is an inspired interpreter, as well as a foreteller, disclosing past, present, and future. *Christ is priest* by offering a sacrifice on our behalf and by making intercession for us to satisfy divine justice. He is our High Priest who reconciles us to a Holy God who demands that sin be punished. Christ was not a sinner, but He became sin for us. This took place in time, but was timeless. He reconciles us to God who started the process by loving us, by ransoming us, by fulfilling the law that we sinners have violated, by sacrificing Himself, and by making continual intercession for us. *Christ is King* in that He triumphs over us, rules over us, and defends us. Prophecies call Him our King and while His kingship is spiritual now, it will be concrete in the future. He will come to total victory and every knee will bow before Him. (PM3).

"The will of man" 1/27/37 (1/5/44). Christianity is not a fatalistic religion like Islam. Though God works in us, man has free will. There are four types of control over man's will: *One is by power.* Christ did not use His power to force us to believe, even though He was tempted to do so. *Another way is by personality.* Jesus tells people to count the cost and not just to follow Him because of His charisma. *Yet another is intellectual influence.* Jesus did not share all secrets with His disciples because they were not yet ready for them. *Lastly, by emotional influence.* In the case of the rich young ruler, Christ could have used emotion to make him follow Him, but He didn't. Judas could have been stopped by the ties of emotion, but Christ didn't use it. Christ respects our freedom of will as individuals. (PM 5).

"World brotherhood and the Bible" 2/37. (PM6).

"Pharisees of today" 3/37. (PM7).

"The value of personal testimony" 3/37. (PM8).

"The enemies of Jesus" 4/29/37 (9/15/43, 4/22/48). (PM9).

"A return to religion" 8/37. (PM10).

"Faith and works" 6/37. (PM11).

"What can a man believe" (A series of talks for fall of 1937). (PM12).

"Communism as a religion" 5/26/37. (PM13).

"Christianity and nationalism – ways to combat nationalism" (No date). (PM14).

"The church in Germany 1933-37" 7/37. (PM15).

"Church and the family" 10/12/38 (5/17/44). (PM16).

"What must I do to be saved?" 1937. (PM17).

"The walks of life" (Boy scouts) (No date). (PM18).

"The character of Jesus" 1937 (2/16/45). (PM19).

"Access to God" 1937 (4/11/45). (PM21).

"Hebrews in history" 1/38. (PM22).

"George Washington – the influence of religion in his life and in the life of the nation" 2/23/38. (PM23).

"The face of Jesus" 2/16/38. (PM24).

"Biblical attitude to women" 12/7/38 (12/8/38). (PM43)

"Marriage in the Bible" 1/26/38. (PM45).

"Value men like that" 2/12/39 (3/22/53, 5/20/53, 10/11/56). (PM47).

"Religious situation in America-pessimistic or optimistic? 2/16/39. (PM48).

"Love creates obedience" 3/1/39 (11/13/46). (PM50).

"Saints in the church today" 3/15/39 (4/5/44). (PM51).

"The assurance of salvation" 2 Peter 1:10, Heb. 6:11. 3/22/39. (PM52).

"Inter-Testament Period" 3/29/39. (PM53).

"The appearance of Christ to three men" 4/12/39. (PM54).

"Love for God" Psalm 116:1. (No date). (PM56).

"The compliments of Jesus" 9/6/39 (11/6/49). (PM60).

"The compliments of Jesus" 9/13/39 (11/20/49). (PM61).

"Giving self to Christ's program" 9/20/39. (PM62).

"Nominal Christians" 9/27/39. (PM63).

"Spiritual Growth" 11/9/39 (1/44, 1/5/50). (PM64).

"Happiness" 1/3/40 (1/23/46). (PM66).

"The church and world peace" 2/7/40. (PM69).

"Service through loving loyalty" John 21:15. 3/11/40. (PM72).

"Ye must be born again" 4/3/40. (PM75).

"Psalm 43" 4/24/40. (PM78).

"Pure religion" 5/8/40. (PM79).

"The importance of the individual" 6/5/40. (PM80).

"Facing reality today" 9/18/40. (PM82).

"Three mottos for living today" 2/28/45 (4/1/47, 12/7/48, 1/1/49, 7/12/54). (PM84).

"Fret not thyself" Ps. 37. 1/10/45 (4/23/53). (PM85).

"The church" 11/27/40. (PM87).

888

"Mary, the mother of Jesus" 12/18/40. (PM88).

"Orphaned missions" 1/8/41. (PM89).

"Forerunner of Hitler" 1/15/41. (PM90).

"The church" 2/12/41. (PM93).

"Prayer meeting study of I, II, III John" 2/19/41. (PM94).

"Pessimism of the present" Zechariah 4:6. 5/7/41 (5/3/45). (PM95).

"Caleb" (no date). (PM97).

"Holy week" 3/31/85. (PM98).

"Enter not into temptation" 4/24/41. (PM99).

"The place of the church in the life of the community" 5/21/41 (10/25/44). (PM100).

"Evangelism" (No date). (PM105).

"Let Jesus come into your heart" 7/16/41 (3/14/46). (PM106).

"The Bible – the book of seven seals" 3/25/42 (1/12/44, 1/18/47, 12/3/47, 9/29/48, 4/14/55). (PM116).

"The seal of our church" 9/23/42 (11/23/44, 3/8/55). (PM126).

"Missionaries on the Gripsholm (a Swedish ship)" 9/30/42. (PM127).

"The resources of the church" 9/30/42. (PM128).

"God reigns" 7/42. (PM132).

"Your tomorrow" 7/1/42 (6/56). (PM133).

"A world in flames" (No date). (PM134).

"Christian fellowship" 1John 1:3-7. 9/16/42 (5/15/49, 9/25/51, 3/1/59). (PM135).

"Evangelism today" 11/17/42. (PM136).

"The church in our community" (No date). (PM137).

"Series on the Christian life" 12/16/42. (PM139).

"Character of the advent" 12/23/42. (PM140).

"Repentance" 1/6/43. (PM141).

"The Christian and giving" 2/10/43. (PM142).

"By what are we known" 10/9/49 (1/9/55). (PM143).

"Race situation in post war world" 2/17/43. (PM144).

"Christian biography series – Dwight L. Moody" 2/24/43 (6/20/46). (PM145).

"Christian biography series – Dr. C.W. Grafton" 3/17/43. (PM147).

"Christian biography series – Mary Slessor of Calabar" 3/24/43 (5/15/46, 1/18/48). (PM148).

"Christian biography series – David Livingstone" 4/7/43. (PM149).

"Larger evangelism" 5/19/43 (1/10/44). (PM149).

"The church as a brotherhood" 6/7/44 (1/8/53). (PM157).

"Take heed, we are followers of God - 1" 3/8/44. (PM161).

"The expression of 'Take heed' as used in Jesus' teaching – 2, 3" 3/14/44 (3/22/44). (PM162).

"Take heed unto thyself - 4" 3/28/44. (PM163).

"Why the church?" 2/16/44. (PM164).

"The men in the service and their church" 2/4/44. (PM165).

"The book of Micah" 12/15/43. (PM166).

"Hosea" 12/8/43. (PM167).

"The book of Nahum" 12/1/43. (PM168).

"The book of Haggai" 11/17/43. (PM170).

"Repentance" 7/12/44 (7/19/44, 8/2/44). (PM172).

"God at work" 11/15/45. (No number).

"Essential to the kingdom" 2/5/48 (12/6/56). (No number).

Tom Frist

"Unconscious influence" Acts 5:29. 1/11/51. (No number).

"Wait on the Lord" 3/11/54. (No number).

"Others" 5/13/54. (No number).

"Plan ahead" 10/6/55. (No number).

NOTES FOR OTHER TALKS

"Words, their importance" (Notes for a Sunday school talk). 9/16/37.

"The art of being a gentleman" (Notes on talk to S.A.E., Sigma Phi, Kappa Sig.). 11/11/37 (2/7/38, 2/28/38, 9/10/40).

"The minister and public speaking" (Outline of a talk delivered to a class in public speaking at Miss. State College). 12/9/37.

"Witnessing" (Notes for Y.M.C.A. retreat). 9/9/38.

"Appearances fool us" 9/26/38 (9/29/38).

"If I were a sophomore" (Outline of talk to the Sophomore Y council). 10/38.

"Obstructionists to the cause of Christ" (Synod talk notes). 1/22/40.

"Notes for a talk to Sigma Phi Epsilon Pledges" 9/20/40.

"Religious education in school life" (Just notes). 3/7/42.

"Loyalty" (Notes for SAE banquet). 3/9/42.

"What are the churches doing about religious work?" (Notes for a Presbytery talk). 4/28/42.

"Jesus—the Light of the world" (Notes for vespers of Y.M.C.A.). 8/9/42.

"Responsibility" (Notes for talk at Miss. State). 10/28/42.

"Comparison of the Bible and the Sears Roebuck catalogue" (Notes for talk at Starkville high school and "the Negro school"). 1/11/43 (7/28/43).

"Troubles and the Christian" 2 Cor. 4:8-17. 2/14/43 (10/7/51).

"Each man and his job" (Notes for talk at Starkville Rotary Club). 7/16/43.

"Service" (Notes for talk at Zonta Club in Tampa). 9/24/43.

"Installation of officers for King's daughters class" (Notes). 10/23/44.

"U.S.O. Mother's day talk" (Notes). 5/13/45.

"Thanksgiving" (Notes for talk at Kiwanis Club). 11/24/48.

"Gratitude" (Notes). 11/25/49.

"Foreign missions" (Notes). 1/29/50.

"Growth in Christian living" (Notes). 4/5/51.

"Christian gratitude" (Notes). 12/13/51.

"Learning to like those we dislike" (Notes). Luke 6:31-36, Romans 12:14-19. 1/10/52 (11/19/57).

"Why we do not receive Jesus and the power of the new life He offers" (Notes). 11/16/52.

"Born from above" (Notes). 11/20/52.

"Christian life, a walk" (Notes). 12/11/52.

"Week of self denial for world missions" (Notes). 1/29/53.

"Happiness" (Notes). 4/10/53.

"He stirred up people" (Notes). 3/26/54.

"Be not weary in well-doing" (Notes). 4/19/51 (10/3/57).

"Sonship of believer" (Notes). John 1:12. 3/11/53.

"My church" (Notes for kick-off for Religious Education Building Fund). 1/27/54.

"There are different motives behind this word 'serve'" (Notes for capping service for nurses aides). 1/28/54.

"Building a better South" (Just notes and no date).

"Doing the disagreeable" (Notes for Miss. State College talk). Matt. 16:24. (No date).

"It's great to be a preacher" (Notes for talks to Kiwanis Club, Rotary Clubs of 5 cities, Junior Chamber of Commerce, Woman's club, Stockton Men's Club, Campus Club). (No date).

"The price of leadership is knowledge and hard work" (Notes). (No date).

"I thirst" John 19:28. (Notes for Good Friday). (No date).

"The state of the church today" (Notes). (No date).

"The individual" (Notes). (No date).

"Christ and world salvation" (Notes). (No date).

"The emergence of the layman" (Notes). (No date).

"Christian family week" (Notes). (No date).

"Heart" (Notes). (No date).

"The missing experience" (Notes). (No date).

"Mirrors of the soul – a study of eight great psalms" (Notes). (No date).

"Value of worship" (Notes). (No date).

"Character building work of Christianity" (Notes). (No date).

****